Radioman:
From a World War to a World Series

Radioman:

From a World War to a World Series

By

Howard F. Stitzel, with
Donald J. Hammond, Jennifer S. Hammond,
& Linda K. Turman

Howard Stitzel's Memoirs from the Pacific to the Detroit Tigers.

Introduction

"I loved working with Stitz for a lot of reasons—his humor, his friendship, his tolerance—but most of all for his dedication to making Tigers broadcasts sound great. He approached his engineering job at the ballpark the way he did everything else in life, with complete dedication to excellence. He's the only man who never wanted (and never had) his voice heard on Tigers broadcasts. And I always loved his straight talk. After all, it was Stitz who informed me of the death of our mutual friend J.P. McCarthy back at Tiger Stadium. I was walking on the field below the broadcast booth when he shouted down, 'Hey Frank, J.P. just kicked the bucket.' Only Stitz could deliver a line like that without anyone taking offense because that's the straight shooter he always was.

Howard Stitzel was one of the most memorable people with whom I've ever worked."

Frank Beckman

Frank Beckman and I in the radio booth at Tiger Stadium.

When we first started thinking about writing Howard's memoir, we pondered what his life had encompassed and realized although his life began with a rather simple start, Howard had lived a storied life with valuable experiences, memories, and stories that might interest others.

Howard Stitzel is not just a gushingly loving grandfather or a caring and committed father and husband, but also part of a World Series Championship and a World War II veteran. Howard saw active duty throughout the "Pacific Theater," as he calls it, but was also a simple farm boy from Pennsylvania, looking for the American Dream. He found it.

Howard is most known for being the trusty radio engineer for the Detroit Tiger Baseball organization in a career that spanned forty-five years. Howard served with radio personalities such as Ernie Harwell, Harry Hielman, Frank Beckman, and George Kell.

Howard is often referred to as "Stitz" by Ernie and others, and was as much a part of Detroit Tiger Baseball as anyone in the booth, for it was Howard who made sure the radio broadcast reached its faithful listeners.

In his stories about Detroit Tiger baseball and working in the booth with Ernie, or serving in the navy during the Second World War as a patrol craft boat radio engineer, Howard retells a sometimes serious and sometimes humorous side of what happened behind the scenes. Howard, in his own affable, plain, and down-home style, brings you right back to those famous and some not-so-famous moments in his life's journey.

This book is a compilation of stories retold by Howard and brought to life through a collaboration of love, laughter, and dedication to a very special man.

Personally, I have never met a more generous, kind, loyal, or selfless man and have been blessed to have learned about gardening (one of Howard's loves), Tiger Baseball, and World War II from such a wonderfully joyful man. I have never seen Howard angry or speak ill of anyone. Howard is truly an example of how one can be blessed with everything in America. Whether he was turning dials with the Tigers or typing on his Morse code machine in the Pacific, Howard was a radioman with a life story. Howard's story will remind you that life's turns are important, but sometimes it's the sidelines that offer just as much.

Howard truly is…*Radioman: From a World War to a World Series.*

I hope you enjoy reading Howard's story as much as we enjoyed writing it.

Don Hammond

I think that most girls would say they had the best grandfather in the world, but I know I do. Whenever we would go over to my grandparents' house, I would run around yelling for my "papa." He was the one adult in the world that would give me his undivided attention, his unconditional love, and let me do anything my heart desired. He would carry me around on a pillow, pull me around the neighborhood in a little red wagon, take me to the penny candy store and give me a dollar to spend, play red light green light in the house, and whenever I spent the night at his house he would tell the greatest bedtime stories.

My papa, Howard Stitzel, is the most loving, dedicated, and honest man I have ever known. He loved his work and he loved his family even more. My grandma June was a stay-at-home mom and a homemaker her whole life. My grandma took great care of their home, the one they still live in today and have lived in for over 50 years. Papa takes care of the outside of their home and tends the most beautiful garden I have ever seen. Papa plants hundreds of tulips and grows Clematis so large and bountiful that master gardeners are jealous. Often, papa grows plants from seeds in his basement in the winter and attends trade shows to give away his wares. You see, he rarely takes anything home from these shows and never spends money on plants but provides for other people, just like he's provided for his family over the past decades. My grandfather has lived his life believing that hard work, loyalty, trust, and love will provide you with everything you need in this world. He is right.

Helping him write this book has opened my eyes to what is important in life, not how big your house is or the fancy car you drive, but caring for the people in your life and appreciating all that you have each and every day.

Jennifer Hammond

From my earliest memories of my dad pulling me in my wagon and going to the corner root beer stand to writing this book, I can honestly say my life has been wonderful because of my father, Howard Stitzel.

My father traveled often with the Detroit Tigers and his homecoming was always something special. I remember going with my mother to Willow Run Airport, waiting for the huge United Plane to land, and watching all the Tiger baseball players walk off the plane, then seeing my dad and running up to give him a big hug. He would bring me home a new Barbie outfit from every city he had traveled to, but the best part was that he had arrived home again.

Basically, I grew up at Tiger Stadium on the corner of Michigan and Trumbull. Every chance we could, my girlfriends and I would go with my dad to the stadium (at least 3 hours before game time so as not to be late), watch the game, goof around, and after the post-game show we would go into the broadcast booth. Inside the booth was like stepping into a secret world filled with personalities, excitement, and golden memories. What good times they were!

I have been truly blessed, but, in gathering my dad's memories, putting them together for this book, this has been a precious gift. Sometimes in our busy lives we don't get the chance to talk to our parents and learn how their life has made them who they are and thus who we are. I have now had that experience. I recommend to anyone reading this, if you still have the chance to talk to your mother or father, sit down and record information to pass on to future generations.

I do hope you enjoy reading my father's story!

Linda Turman

Table of Contents

Part 1

From the Farm to the Pacific

My Younger Years

My story begins when I was a youngster on the farm in Berks County, Pennsylvania, in Richmond Township, outside a small town with a population of five thousand called Fleetwood. My mother was Jennie Rothmel Hieter Stitzel. She was a quiet person and a hard worker on the farm. Gender didn't mean a thing on the farm—we all had to work hard. My mother would cook for the family and the hired help at harvest time; at times we had as many as twelve mouths to feed. Once in a while a stray old person would pass by, and my mother would insist that he sit with the family and eat with us.

My father was George Sawyer Stitzel. He was tall, strong, gentle, and very strict. He knew all about growing crops and the timing for planting and harvesting. He knew how to fix a broken piece of farm machinery and how to care for the animals. Sometimes he would be the veterinarian and help with the birth of animals at home and other surrounding farms. My hat goes off to my father forever. He was a good man.

My family from Pennsylvania: Susan Sproesser, Jennie Stitzel (my mother), Robert Stitzel (my brother), Arlene Stitzel (my sister), Pearl Sproesser, Rebecca Stitzel, and Frank Stitzel.

The first born to Jennie and George was a girl, named Arlene. She was the second mother to all us kids. Arlene was smart and wound up getting a Bachelor of Science degree from Kutztown State College. She married Walter Miller and had one child, and her name was Katherine Louise Miller. Her nickname was Kitty Lou.

The second born was a boy, Robert Paul Stitzel. He was a very good-looking man. Robert was big and smart and worked on the farm but was always gentle to us youngsters. His ambition in life was to be a pilot, and he was always seen at Wander Field Airport, just to be among his idols. During World War II, being fluent in German Robert served as an interpreter for the German POWs who were stationed in Kutztown, Pennsylvania. Robert had a physical defect (he was hard of hearing) and was rejected from the service, so he never served in the war.

Their third child was a boy, Walter John Stitzel. Walter was also very good-looking and gentle, not to mention sociable and smart. He was hard working like the rest of the family and always got along with everyone. After a time, Walter did not enjoy the farm work, so he migrated to Wyoming and got a job branding cattle until the war started. He served directly under General MacArthur, but while in Australia, Walter got malaria and was discharged and sent home. He had a layover on the West Coast, and in the barracks, his bunker was on the second floor. Because of the malaria, he had to sit near a window and breathe fresh air. At some point he blacked out, and later the official report to my mother was that Walter had blacked out, fell, and died on the spot. My mother got the U.S. flag with one star. Our family always cherished that flag and the memory of Walter.

I was their fourth child, Howard Franklin Stitzel. Of course, I was my mother's favorite, and I always made her laugh. I can remember how when I was young, I was afraid of Santa Claus, otherwise known as Belsnickel by the Pennsylvania Dutch. The neighbor would always dress up as Santa, and I would get coal from Santa for my present. None of the other kids got coal, just me. It was because I was afraid and hiding under the kitchen table waiting for my sweet mother to save me, but only after she had a good laugh.

Jennie and George's fifth child was a daughter named Violet. She helped my mother in the house, as did other girls her age. She followed our sister Arlene into teaching and also graduated from

Kutztown State College. Violet became a third grade teacher, and she loved her students. She married Warren Frey and they had a daughter, Warrene Frey, and a son who is my namesake, Howard George Frey. He is big, strong, good-looking, and gentle.

My sister, Violet, and I one day while I was on leave from the U.S. Navy.

In our world on the farm, we were normal country people. There was never much money. We all wore hand-me-downs, but we worked hard and we loved one another. We sold the vegetables from our gardens, we got along well with our neighbors, and we lived in a community where everyone always helped one another. I loved my family, and I believe that my parents' influence in my upbringing helped shape the person I am today.

The Stitzel farm in Fleetwood, Pennsylvania.

My schooling took place in a rural red schoolhouse. Mrs. Merkel was my teacher from first to eighth grade. Every day I had to walk two miles to get there, and in winter I did the same thing, only with heavier clothing while treading through four feet of snow, never missing a day.

In the summertime my duty to the farm was plowing. That is, two horses pulled the plow and I walked in the furrow behind them, planting corn, oats, and alfalfa. I helped my mom in the garden whenever she saw me loafing somewhere—sometimes I would hide and smoke one of Uncle Frank's cigarettes, or corn silk when no cigs were available. At the age of ten, in fifth grade, I would sit under bridges and smoke a cig, and one time Mrs. Merkel smelled me and put me in the coal cellar until it was time to go home.

When I went to Fleetwood High School, I managed through the courses, and for some reason I aced algebra, trigonometry, and geometry. I flunked civics, French, and got a C in English. I hated to go to school; I did my chores every day from five a.m. to seven a.m., being sure to get to school by eight. I milked the cows, cleaned the cow, horse, and pig waste and everything else that needed to be done on the farm. Then one day the Bond Bread truck man told me they needed a salesman, so I got the job and had fun, especially wooing the gals on the route.

That ended when I enlisted in the navy.

Introduction to the Navy

My brother Walter was the fourth conscription number out of the fish bowl. When World War II started, the officials loaded a fish bowl with one thousand numbers and blindfolded someone to select numbers which were associated with names; those boys were the first to be called to duty. My brother Walter was called in the fourth round. I had a good talk with him when he came home on a leave from the army. He told me he trained in mud, snow, under barbed wire fence, and live bullets came flying three feet over his head. I immediately told myself that that was not for me—so he advised me to join the navy immediately.

After I signed up for the navy, the lieutenant told me to go home and wait for my call to duty. March came around, and sure enough, I got a letter—it said report to war. I signed my commitment and was shipped to Providence, Rhode Island, for naval training base boot camp. It was the place where you had to pass many tests and physical exams. We were issued navy clothes at camp, including shoes and leggings, which held your pants close to your ankles so you wouldn't trip while marching. The captain told us to line up in fours for our marching drills, which seemed to last forever on that drill field.

Here I am wearing my uniform proudly.

I still remember the hospital on the base with the doctors who'd make you suck soap if you didn't obey them. Two doctors had our company men line up single file to pass the needles. There was one doctor on each side, so you couldn't avoid the tetanus shots. I remember there was one boy who stood six feet, six inches tall, and when the needles hit his shoulder, he cringed, took a step, and fell flat on his face. That's how the navy affected tough guys. Then it was my turn, and so the ugly doctors injected the tetanus needles. I didn't even feel the injections and just walked away. Low and behold, five steps ahead of me was another doctor with gloves on, and said, "Come here, shorty." This was short-arm inspection.

Another test in the navy was swimming. In order to save ourselves in the open ocean, we had to know how to swim, so my company and I marched down to the pool for the test. I had never seen a pool that big in all my life. The lieutenant got behind me and told me to jump in and swim a hundred yards. I got scared at about fifty and started to sink. Someone came along on the side of the pool with a hook, grabbed my body, and pulled me the next fifty yards. At the end, I was told I passed the test, and every boot (a soldier, that is) that was looking started laughing.

My next orders were to report to radio signal school in Noroton Heights, Connecticut. We all had bunks in the barracks at the radio school, and at six a.m. every morning the bullhorns woke us up. We'd go to the mess hall for chow and would be off to the classroom after that. There I got a pair of earphones and listened and learned the dots and dashes of International Morse Code. By the third day in the classroom, we had to write a letter while listening to Morse code. I listened for two weeks and tried to write the "dit-daw-dit-daw-dit-dit-dit." I was scared that if I didn't pass the test, they'd keep me in that classroom until I did. It took me three weeks, but then in a flash out of the blue, it all seemed to be easy, and I was assigned to New York Pier 92.

Once on Pier 92, there was a crowd of boots waiting for assignment. There were many men waiting for their names to be called. I waited six days. Then, on that sixth day, the commander of the pier told me to go to the recreation area and handed me a pair of official boxing gloves, directing me up to the boxing ring. They wanted to see how well I could box against the guy waiting for me. The gloves were big and heavy. I didn't even get them up in front of my face before my opponent threw one punch and I went down. My opponent was Schlizzy, and to me, he appeared to be a welterweight champion. Now you know that a farmer and a boxer just don't mix.

Another time I went back to the bunk with the rest of my company, and we had an assignment waiting for us. That night we had to dress properly, with leggings, a belt, and a .45 pistol. The six of us marched two piers down to the *SS Normandie*. During WWII, she was seized by the U.S. authorities in New York and renamed the *USS. Lafayette*. In 1942, she caught fire and capsized onto her portside in the mud of the Hudson River. The luxury liner was lying on her side between the piers. The carpenters from New York City had built a four-foot-wide walkway on the ship's side. The lieutenant assigned our group to walk up and down the length of the *SS Normandie*, and if anyone looked suspicious, we were to tell them to halt. If they didn't halt, we were told to shoot to kill. Nothing exciting happened during my watch. I never had a reason to use my weapon in the navy—well, except for target practice, and this made me a very happy man.

Away from home, I grew a beard and did my best to look the part of a sailor.

Out to Sea

Then they assigned me to a ship, which meant no more shore duty for three years, eight months, and thirteen days. On board, our first assignment for the PC548 (patrol craft) was to escort a convoy to Gitmo and watch for U-boats. Then we were assigned to Port of Spain, Trinidad, with other PC boats. From there we went to Coco Solo, Christoble, Panama, and the canal to San Diego. We headed west. I don't think we missed a single atoll or small island in the Pacific war zone. We were always on convoy duty.

Some crew members of the PC548 gather for a picture, with me hanging out in the background.

We were on patrol in Hawaii when we brought in the USS PC 548 for dry-dock duty. It took two weeks to chip paint and repair the underwater QCQ equipment. QCQ was the sound detector that told you a submarine was in the area, signaling you to press the button to call all hands to their battle stations. The PC 548 didn't have any assigned convoy duty at the time, so the navy command gave us the job to protect the entrance to Pearl Harbor for about five days. To my surprise, there was a lull in the message department that week, so every night I'd put my headphones on and with one ear listen to KGU AM—the civilian broadcast from Oahu. KGU AM was the most pleasant station of the whole war because it would play ukulele music during the nights for the late listeners. On slow nights I'd tell all the hands in earshot of the KGU signal that there was no music that compared to Hawaiian ukulele music. The only one that came close, in my opinion, was WSM Nashville and the country songs they played, like Hank Williams, Sr. and Eddie Arnold. Eventually, we got an assignment to get underway, so we gave the new USS PC 548 a once-over and went out to sea.

Night scenes in the middle of the Pacific Ocean were beautiful. On the nights I could get off the four-hour radio shack work duty, I would watch the water; I saw where the bow of the ship pushed the ocean away on both the starboard and the portside. If you looked down, even in that disturbance, you'd see what I saw—that ocean water has a phosphorescent quality to it. There were about five feet of sparkles on either side of the ship. It looked like the white lights of Christmas.

The quartermaster would come out on occasion to start sightings and tell the captain where we exactly were in the Pacific at that time of day or night. Gould was our quartermaster, and he did a fine job with his sextant and chronometer. He got us to our destinations in the vast Pacific Ocean without any incident, and we appreciated such accuracy.

There are a million different jobs in the navy that don't get recognized. Think of the deck hand and the swab jockeys—both are important. Coxswains and boatmen's mates are signalmen who flash their lights when we run radio silence—they're important, too. The cook onboard PC 548, Altair, was the only one everyone appreciated. When the ocean waves were high and mighty, the galley was not the place to be. Dishes, pots, and pans fell off shelves and food spilled all over the galley deck, but Altair wouldn't grumble. He'd clean up the mess, and when chow time came around, Altair had it ready. As a radioman onboard, I never had to peel potatoes or do other K.P. (kitchen patrol) duty because we could not get our fingers dirty. On that note, I must also commend the below deck crew, the guys known as the bilge ostriches. They were always sweaty and greasy. When we were down by the equator, the bilge ostriches would come to the top to cool off, since they only had fans below deck, where the heat was unbearable. They repeatedly had to go to the doctor for heat pimples and scabs from the temperatures. They, too, were appreciated.

When we, the radiomen, wanted to start a fight, we would open the hatch to the engine room and yell down, "How are ya, bilge ostriches?" We'd have to duck immediately because they would try to hit us with a barrage of wrenches from their work pouches. They never got me! But on the other side of the coin, the engine crew was a bunch of the nicest guys who went with us on shore passes. We would pick a fight with the gyrenes (G.I. + marine = gyrene), and the men in the engine room were the best fighters ever.

Quartermaster Gould (middle), Chief Radioman Joe Clark (right) and I (left) smiling at the camera as we head out to the Pacific.

The Order of the Deep

We were in the Atlantic and heading for New York with a convoy from Gitmo, and believe me—no ship ever passes Cape Hatteras without going through high waves and choppy waters. I had to sit in the radio shack with my knees buckled for one wave, and I'd have to straighten them back out as the ship rolled onto the next. At times my typewriter went from my nose to six feet away. We expected those conditions on board because Cape Hatteras is where warm currents meet the cold northern seawater. When we came to Ambrose Lightship outside New York Harbor, I had a ping return—there was a U-boat ahead. We were the lead boat in the convoy, and so we hit the U-boat with a depth charge, but the senior officer present at action (SOPA) gave the signal light to move out. He took over, and we hit it with our little bombs, called cans, and got one U-boat at the Ambrose Lightship.

After our convoy got to Gitmo, we got an assignment in the Pacific. We tied up in the Port of Spain in Trinidad to refuel and outboard to a hospital ship. I have never seen so many hurt sailors like we saw on that ship. Going through the canal, we followed an unknown freighter and rode the highs and lows of the water level as the gates opened to another level. The water was low, twelve feet down from the pulling tram, and all small ships had to anchor themselves to keep in line. One time I had my own duty in anchoring; stationed on the starboard side of the bow, I was attached to the ship with a heaving line, looking straight up. The captain had told me, "Be sure you hit the receiver." The receiver is the sailor standing on the dock catching the line. All engines had stopped, and with all hands watching from the bridge, I upped the heaving line and let it go and I hit the receiving guy right in the gut. I got a barrage from the captain. Oops.

We were headed to San Diego when a storm came up, and we were ordered to take refuge in a small town in Mexico. We were the third PC boat to get into the sheltered bay, and we tied up to each other. We spent the night there and five of us got so drunk that in the morning we didn't want to walk the six-by-two plank from the flying bridge to PC 548. I guess I was lucky because I didn't know that the ships had been bobbing at anchor. I have no recollection of crossing, but somehow I did it and was off to San Diego.

In San Diego we came back from a shakedown to San Clemente. A shakedown is when new sailors come aboard ship and begin to learn their new duties. That's where I spotted a huge carpet fish that measured about twenty-five feet by twenty-five feet, right under the bow. Coming back to our assigned pier, the captain made some big mistakes. We came too close to a mini-carrier, known as a flat top, already anchored and our yardarm hit the below deck mounts, twisting the mast off. We all snickered at this. Then we proceeded to the pier and had another mistake. The bow hit the pier because someone on the bridge or the engine room gave the signal to move forward instead of reverse. The commanding admiral was on the pier and witnessed the incident. He had been only six feet from our bow and barely jumped out of the way. We didn't laugh then.

Our next port was the famous Pearl Harbor. Our boss for the Pacific U.S. Navy command for the radio signal was NPM—all official directions came from Washington's Naval Communication Station (NSS), so when I heard a call, it would say: "USS PC 548, this is NSS." My hands would shake, but I got through it.

We had lots of time in Honolulu because we had repairs, barnacle scrapes, and painting for the PC 548. We would get patrol duty up and down the entrance of the harbor, and I'd listen for messages in one ear and listen to the sweet summer night Hawaiian music in the other. I'd do this all through my four hours on duty and eight hours off. Anywhere we went on this watch schedule, I'd also listen and copy news from Tokyo Rose on a typewriter with twelve onionskin sheets to make a newsletter for the sailors, then I'd copy Vladivostok, a Russian radio station, to get some friendly news.

In our travels, we took a convoy to Alaska and found out just how tough an ocean can be, even with no wind. The waters on sunny days had waves that were twenty, twenty-five feet high, and the PC would roll and jump, slamming nose first into the big ones. The waves covered everything up to the flying bridge, and when they passed, we'd pop out of the waves. After we had hit Attu, Kiska, and Sitka, we were all glad to go back to the war zone in the mid-Pacific. Whenever our convoy went west, the quartermaster would announce, "We are now going into tomorrow, and when we return, we will be coming into yesterday." When we had crossed the equator near tomorrow, all the rookies, commonly known as polliwogs, who were aboard for their first time across had to be initiated into "King Neptune's Order of the Deep." So all hands would bring buckets of garbage, urine, and oil, and dump it into a miniature swim pool. We had to dive into four feet of water full of shit and galley waste and get to the other side of the swimming pool. I officially became a shellback and a member of the Order of the Deep.

My official certification to prove I am a member of The Order of the Deep.

A sailor getting ready to be commissioned to The Order of the Deep.

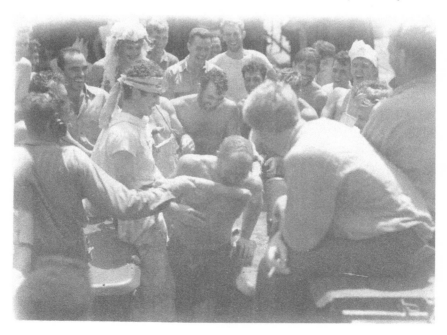

This sailor was just initiated. Looks fun, doesn't it?

A group of sailors surround the tub of waste to help initiate the new sailors.

The Pacific

We were on a convoy to Christmas Island, the place where bombers took off and landed for raids on Tokyo. Our PC 548 had been assigned "hook duty" for three days. When bombers approached land but had a wheel up or something else wrong, they weren't able to stop, often overshooting the landing strip. Our job was to fish out pilots that had made it out of the bomber and were splashing in the water. We hooked the men before sharks fed on them. Otherwise, the sharks had a feast. The PC 548 was on an aircraft frequency, so we knew when bombers were about to land. We'd see the splash and the men scrambling, so the captain would give the order, "Full speed ahead," toward the soldiers in the water. We'd spot one or two pilots, hook them, and bring them on board. There were so many sharks there that we knew if we didn't get the men out of the water after two minutes, they were fish food.

The PC548 crew casually hanging out. For most of our travels, we were not required to wear our official uniforms.

We convoyed once to Kwajalein and Eniwetok, where there were dogfights and the night skies were always lit up with searchlights. The Japanese would come to bomb the installations on these air raids. They came from one of the islands the U.S. never knew about, Truk Island, only 150 miles from Kwajalein. The fighting continued night after night. Just to let you know, the PC 548 never came close to a bomb. The word was that we were too small and unimportant; we would have been a waste of a bomb for the Japanese. Now you can tell just how lucky I was to have been on the safest ship in the navy.

One convoy took us to Saipan, Tinia, and Guam. We would be inside lagoons with our communication officer on board, listening to the thud, the alert whistles from the battleships and guns overhead. We were the directorial ship for landing small boats; it was a sight to see, checking our starboard side and seeing as many as thirty loaded boats depositing marines on the beach. I can still hear the big guns projecting overhead. It excited me, yet I was never nervous at any time.

Another time when we convoyed to Guam, we raised the Union Jack (the English flag), indicating we were not at war as long as the flag was flying, behind the mine net (a net where submarines could not get behind, it was considered a safe zone), and stayed there without the threat of danger. Looking at a mountain in the distance, we saw plumes of smoke from enemy fire rise out of holes in the rock. We knew we were out of range of other crafts, so we went back into the galley and had supper. On Saturdays, our cook, Altair, made what was commonly known as S.O.S. (Shit on a Shingle), but it was really the best beef tips on toast I've ever tasted. This particular Saturday, Altair made extra. We all had three good-sized helpings followed by a good smoke. Then one guy got out his cards, took all of our money, and said thank you.

There were other times when we wouldn't have any orders with convoys, so we'd head to our appointed destinations, sometimes in smooth waters on the equator. Some fellows took naps topside, in the shade of our three-inch gun. The sun would beam down, and with no wind, the sea was smooth as glass. One fellow slept so soundly that when the ship changed course, the sun burned nearly half of his body. We only wore shorts and never had captain's inspection en route to somewhere. I would take my turn on the four-on and eight-off stretch and gaze down at the phosphorescent lights in the middle of nowhere.

The PC boat was a small and tough craft. It was easiest to steer it when the waves came at us head-on. The other way to fight the sea was to aim in the direction of the waves as they slammed into our stern. Likely they were pushing us along the coastline, often about twenty miles offshore. The waves would lift our stern clear out of the water, but after the crest of the wave went by, the stern and the crew would be operating again. The bow may have bounced day and night high above the water, creaking here and there, but the men and women in Bay City, Michigan, are to be complimented for the toughness of the PCs they produced. I want to thank all of the shipbuilders for making that sturdy ship. Even if it did moan and groan on the sea, not a drop of salt water got into a compartment on board.

The navy was where I learned to work with people. I learned there were big shots with bars on their shoulders; I learned respect. On that boat, I never got seasick, even going through three tsunamis. In the navy, I learned to keep my cool, no matter where or when.

My official photograph for the U.S. Navy.

Letter to Mom from the War

I sent this letter to my mother while I was in the navy. I missed my family dearly and loved hearing from them while in the service. You can tell from my letter that I wanted to know what was happening at home, how my brother Walter was doing in the service, and how important it was for me to help my family even when I was at war.

Dear Mom:

I have a lot of time on my hands, and I can think of no better way to keep myself busy than to write a couple of lines. I have not been making out so well with the bundles of heaven (girls) around here this year; I think they grew to be sort of snooty. So instead of hanging around town becoming more and more disgusted each time I go on liberty, I just keep my nose clean and try to pick up a few nice Christmas presents, just in case I am able to bring them home personally. I just do not know whether a relief will come for me, at present, but I have been told that within the sort-of-near future I will be able to see the States again. And when I do, I will grab the first plane home. If you can send me a letter real quick and write some suggestions "what I would like for Christmas," I would surely appreciate them. And if the finances will hold out, I will get them for you (Pop, I cannot take an asiangirl home) so that lets you open to make other suggestions.

I attended church last Sunday for the first time in almost one year, and I sort of felt funny and out of place with no one to sit aside of like Arlene or Mom. Remember Mom, when I came up to see you once when you were in church? I sure wish I could do that again. When was the last time that you have had communion? I did not get communion here; I don't think they do those things, or this was just one occasion when they didn't. I still have a church bulletin, and I will either bring it home or send it to you to see.

I called up Avis Koller's landlady, and she told me that Avis had gotten herself a job in Reading. Have you ever met her? I mean Avis. I suppose she is living with her parents now; will you please ask Pop to go out there and give my best regards to the whole family. Mrs. Reeves (the landlady) told me also that Clyde Lesher had visited not very long ago, and that he was going back to the States on rotation program.

I am stopping off my allotment (pay) for the time being, just to make myself available to some Mazuma (drink), since I am in port now and have the chance to get Four Roses whiskey. I am helping myself to all that I can. Please don't worry, I know when I have had enough. So far the shore patrols have not caught up with me, and I think they won't. If the allotment is stopped off, I will get my whole pay, and then I can adjust myself to fast living and things. I do also want to have the money coming to me here just in case I am able to get back to the States; then I'll have enough to get a plane ticket. I hear that we are going to get thirty days leave and ten or less days traveling time. Gee, I am excited even though I don't know whether I will be able to come home. There are about four sailors leaving the ship that are living around the East Coast who might stop in for schnapps. I hope you have a good stock on hand. Just be sure that you do supply up, in case I get there. I'll make up for the year of hell that is past now.

I am only sorry that Walter cannot come home when I do. He should be somewhere around Hollandia in New Guinea or maybe still further in the Philippines. I sure hope he gets to stay in the second line instead of at the front. I haven't heard from him now for about a month. I guess he is busy as all hell. I know that he would write to me if he wasn't. Has he mentioned anything to you where he might be? Did he drop any hints? Where do you guess that he is? Please tell me what his general topic of conversation is and don't spare the details.

How are the hunters making out this year with all the rabbits and pheasants? Did Frank get the limit yet? How many did Pop shoot? And how did John make out? Did he clip any off in the orchard? Were there any other hunters up on the farm from Reading? Did Leon Bortz come up this year? Did Hank Lawson or Gloomy or any of the bunch come up there? By the way, where are they right now? If my memory is correct, they were somewhere in the West, in a defense plant. Did Rob and Eva hear from Gloomy lately? They used to be big pals. I am surprised that Hank hasn't written to me. He should know my address. Did Oscar Brown ever come up to see you? He will be there soon if he hasn't been there yet. Tell him that Altare, Sontag, Boots, and almost all the old gang left already. The only reason that I haven't is because there is just no relief available. Tell him that Rovota left also. Did anyone around Fleetwood have any accidents this year with the shooting irons? I mean, did anyone get hurt while rabbit hunting?

Have you had any cold weather yet? Gee, when I get home, I guess everything will be just snowed shut. Imagine me after spending almost a whole year on the equator. I guess I will freeze into an icicle. I'll drop out of a parachute off a plane and when you see me jump, have a good fire in the stove or a good shot of whiskey ready. Gee, I can just imagine me coming home and having the whole damn family in our house and all sitting around the piano with Arlene playing. And when she gets tired, Violet can pinch-hit for her and we all sing the songs like the good ole days. I really have developed a splendid voice. Won't you be surprised! O-LE-O-Lade-O-one of the hillbilly songs, you'll really like.

How is Arlene? Tell her to keep in shape. Lately they have been giving me high hopes to keeping the one date that I am looking forward to when I get home. I do not know what I will do when I get my leave, as far as the dating the broads (girls) are concerned. I will have to just take it all in as it comes. Are the women pretty sociable right now at home? I had been doing all right when I was there, and so I think that I will be able to make out all right when I get there again. Gee, I get so excited when I think of coming home. Believe me, all is being done to get me a leave. And I'll bet you all a dollar that I'll be seeing you in the near future. I'll call you up from San Francisco just as soon as I land. And that can't be soon enough for me.

Please don't be angry with me for stopping off the allotment. I am only doing it so I have more money on hand for different occasions as they arise. And please believe me that I don't spend very much money on drinks. I do know how to take care of myself. I do also hope that stopping off the allotment will not do too much damage or should I say re-figuring out your budget. Please let me know immediately if you cannot get along without it. It is only a small matter to me, but if it means a great deal to you mom, I will send you all the money that you want. Since I am making more now, I am able to send you more monthly in the event that you do need it.

Please don't be afraid to ask, since I have been away from home and have seen all the bad side of the world and the bad things that even you and no one at home would imagine. I realize that you have done so much more for me than I can ever repay.

Be seeing you soon, I hope.

Love to all, Howard.

My beautiful mother, Jennifer Hieter Stitzel

My mother and I walking into the 1940's World's Fair in New York City.

Patrolling Paradise

The USS PC 548 was scheduled for dry dock in Hawaii so we could scrape barnacles and chip paint and repair anything that needed repairing. We were told to go here, there, and somewhere else until the harbormaster got on the horn and told us where the dry dock was. It looked just like any normal pier anchorage until we found ourselves in what felt like a big washtub. The water pumped out of its enclosure, and we saw divers going about and handling four-by-four logs and diving under the ship. They were "making horses," so the keel of the PC 548 was standing in free air as all the water pumped out. The reason for the horses was so people could go standing up under the ship's keel.

The PC548 in drydock.

We were scheduled for three weeks of leave in Honolulu after a couple of months looking at water and coconut trees on the atolls. This is where we took our convoys to the islands on our adventures. Soon the islands looked all alike—all shot up with bare sand. It was a wonderful relief just to get off the ship. We all had loads of money and didn't know how to blow it. We soon found out in the city.

When we finally got off the boat in dry dock and on land (to you landlubbers), the first stop we made in the big city was city hall, where King Kamehameha stood on his pedestal with his royal crown and only a loincloth a king would wear. It all looked so real even though it was a statue. The next thing the sailors on shore leave did was look for girls. Now we had a problem: there was one girl to every two hundred sailors, and I didn't stand a chance with only two stripes showing—I was a radio man, second class. Come to think of it, I thought I was a big cheese at the time, but I soon found out I was only a small-timer compared to those guys in dress-blue uniforms and the old salts with four and five hash marks. So I grumbled and walked somewhere else.

I am standing in Honolulu in front of the statue of King Kamehameha.

Normally we would hit a bar and blow our money in no time flat. We did this almost too fast because one time we could not even pay for a steak dinner. Luckily the old salts (who were broke too) came along and said come on, let's eat. So we all went to a mansion just east of Diamond Head that had a sign on the front gate that read: "All Service Men Welcome." Our hostess was the richest woman in the U.S. at the time—Doris Duke Cromwell. There was a dining room at her home, which was named "Shangri La," with all the good food you could think of. "Help yourselves," the big sign said, so I gobbled so much food that for the first time in my life I got a bellyache and had to stop pigging out.

My buddies and I on liberty in Hawaii, I loved the smell of the flowers.

A group of us posing for a picture at Doris Duke Cromwell's lavish estate.

About a mile from the mansion were the southwest rocky cliffs where the ocean waves had eaten away from the rocks and made a peephole. It was called the blowhole. Every time a large wave would hit the rocks, water would come out through the peephole in a twenty-five-foot spray geyser. It was like taking a mouthful of as much water as your mouth could hold, lying down on your back and looking skyward, and then all of a sudden having to sneeze.

We went back to the city, and the old-timers told us to take the bus to Konchoe Bay across the mountain. The mountain pass was called the "Pali." Our eyes bugged out when we saw the girls there. We whistled and soon found out that we could look but not touch. When we left the King Kamehameha site we had to cross a mountain with a river just alongside of the road. Sometimes, when the west wind was strong enough, the water in the river would go uphill. That is the only place on earth where a river flows backwards.

So we walked on and saw lots of odd things. Once we went ice skating at Pineapple Farms. We grabbed a cab and the cabbie said there was a skating rink up in the Pineapple Farms, and sure enough there was a small 200-foot frozen rink. We went ice skating in the tropics.

Morse Code

Hey, can all you Sparkies (radiomen during the war) out there still read this Morse code message?

.----.. .---. ... .-- .... .-. ...-. .... .-- ... .---.. .---. .-----

My official salute as a member of the U.S. Navy.

This is an International Morse Code refresher. It took me two years of stumbling, but I worked my Morse code key to thirty-five words per minute, and I loved it. I hope all the ex-Sparkies get the message. To send and receive messages, we had the Hallicrafter, an all-band radio receiver, and in the middle of the Pacific Ocean, the signal that we copied would sometimes fade out from KMPC in Honolulu. Then, we had to be sure the superherodine signal from Washington, D.C., was tuned to the frequency we were copying.

Inside the radio room onboard the ship, we had about eight feet of space. We sometimes had to turn the receiver to get a high pitch on the headsets, which made it louder. In rough water, we had to copy the five-letter encrypted message, and the ship rocked and rolled so much that I had to spread my feet apart and balance the typewriter. Sometimes the typewriter would be six inches from my nose, and the next wave would drop it down by my knees. The Hallicrafter drifted at the same time, so we'd use our spare hands to tune in to get maximum receiving signal. When we were on the other side of the dateline and far away from the command signal, and if there was a storm nearby, it was almost impossible to get all five letters right. If one were missing, Mr. Emery, our executive officer, would say to us what Captain Weed would concur: "Don't worry, Sparkie, it cleared almost all the mistakes." It was by way of the Haglin decoder machine and the strip boards that the officers figured out what the message was, because in the end, the words would come out of the Haglin machine in readable, plain language. Just in case we were captured, the secrets would not get out because the Sparkies never knew what the message said; our job was to type the Morse code, not to read it.

Leaving Active Duty

Once, when the USS PC 548 had an escort to Midway, we didn't get into any rough water. We then moored at the dock and were told we had three days to chase gooney birds off the airplane runway so that they wouldn't get into the engine motors when the planes landed. That got monotonous quickly, so we went to shallow water at the end of the strip at Midway and saw landmines ahead of us. Crazy as it seems, some of the landlubber sailors on their off-duty time were jumping from one hot mine to the other. That amazed me! We wound up jumping on them too. The mines were hot but weren't working, so we kept on jumping from one to the next. Eventually this became dull, and we turned our attention to shelling. One sailor told us that there were shell animals that got between the mine plates at high tide and couldn't get out during low tide so they died there and crystallized. There was one unique shell animal with an eye that closed when another seashell animal came close by. That eye in Midway shallow waters was green, and during the war you could get as high as five dollars per eye. I wound up with a shoebox full. Then, later on, when we were assembled and had to flake out all of our possessions in our traveling sea bags, the captain in charge said, "All you can take home was what you were issued when you entered the navy." We could take home our pea coat, Alaska foul weather gear, and the shoes that were on our feet. My gripe of this story is that I could not take home the box full of cats' eyes, the unclaimed diamond rings I found in the bottom of a mail bag, my .45 pistol, and my assigned Tommy gun and volt-ohm analyzer. The sailor next to me said, "Why are you so dumb, Howard? You're an honest man, but besides, you should have mailed that home before inspection." I always find out the secrets too late.

On break, walking the streets enjoying the Earth beneath my feet.

In November 1945, I was honorably discharged from the United States Navy.

Finally, in Guam I caught a Naval Air Transport Service (NATS) plane to San Pedro and then off east to a hospital base in El Paso, on the Texas-Mexico border. There I was kicked off the NATS plane to make way for wounded sailors, which I never regretted and with twenty-five dollars in my pocket, I kept trying to get out of El Paso for three days. To my surprise, a Chinese pilot had seen me and asked if I wanted a ride east. I had to get on a twin-engine black widow plane, and he said it was against the rules. I said it was okay by me. So off we went east to Cincinnati. I then took a bus to Fleetwood, Pennsylvania to visit my family, before reporting to the radio school at the Ford Rouge Plant off Schaffer Road in Dearborn, Michigan, where they were building and testing the buzz bomb.

On one of my night leaves, I was chasing girls, and of all the luck, I met my wife June and have been blessed ever since. Now I brag about my life. I have one daughter, Linda, two granddaughters, Jennifer and Amy, and maybe a sailor-to-be, my great-grandson, Jacob. With them my story continues.

Part 2

My Major League Baseball Experience

My Radio Career in the "Off" Season

My work in the broadcast industry began in Allentown, Pennsylvania, at WKAP. I had become an audio engineer after I got out of the navy and radio school (RETS: radio electronics school), and my duties were remotes, studio, disc cutting, and the *Man on the Street* interviews, as well as the transmitter watch. It was through this industry that I met and worked with a score of people and made memories I've kept to this day.

It was later that my wife June and I moved to Detroit. After two days of job hunting, I began at Tiger Stadium with Harry Heilmann and the baseball broadcasts. We covered the whole Midwest with the Tigers broadcasts. I got the radio job in Detroit in five minutes. Harry Heilmann was the announcer for the Detroit Tigers at the time. The chief engineer at WJBK AM called me to the booth, and I set up the equipment, like the job I had in Allentown. The top of the first inning went by fast, and then I felt a hand on my shoulder. The chief said, "I'll see you later. You've got the job." Except for the games where Paul and Ernie went without an engineer, I had that job with the Tigers starting in 1948.

Heilmann used to do ticker tape reconstruction when the Tigers were on the road, and he decided that he wanted to do all the games home and away. So he picked me for the job, and I got to go to spring training with the team. Imagine going to Florida, watching a ball game, and getting a salary for it! There was no satellite when we went to spring training in 1951. There was just a pair of wires from my amplifier to the telephone pole connection, like a phone line. I had a card table and my little transistor amplifier on top of the home dugout. Sometimes it would get hot and noisy because of the players in Lakeland. My job was to turn two buttons, and that's been my whole career in broadcasting. Imagine that.

I would do studio work and remotes in the off-season. I taped a couple of shows for the Gentile and Binge shows. One was the "Headless Horseman" and the other one was *"Beautiful Carl."* That was the funniest radio show in Detroit for at least ten years. I also recorded classical symphonic music for Karl Haas, a WWJ Detroit classical music host, and sent it out to ten stations throughout the country. Later, the key broadcast station changed from WJBK to WKMH, with the *Bobbin' with Robin Show*, and *Swinging Time with Robin Seymore* in Detroit was born. Other personalities I worked with were Marty McNeely, Frank Simms, and Dick Purtan.

I did football games with Van Patrick and Bob Reynolds, including University of Michigan and Michigan State University games. I also did hockey teams from Toronto, with Foster Hewitt Sr., and Montreal, broadcasting in both English and French simultaneously. I had to broadcast in French because the engineer who was supposed to do it didn't show; I was the engineer with French in one ear and English in the other. When I heard the French say "Detroit," it meant commercial time, which also meant it was time out for English, and when my stopwatch said one minute thirty seconds—the signal for both languages—it all worked out.

After a while, the WJBK key station became WJR, and naturally I followed. I did studio work, remotes, and baseball for WJR. I worked with J. P. McCarthy, the radio personality, in the studio and on remote at his scheduled golf course shows. I worked on football games with Van Patrick and Bob Reynolds. At Tiger Stadium (when the Detroit Lions played there), our assigned booth was in the third deck on the fifty-yard line, next to the public address booth with Joe and Larry Gentile, public address announcers for the Detroit Lions. We were exposed to the cold weather. The wind would come across the roof at twenty-eight degrees. To me it felt like the coldest spot on earth.

Working the JP McCarthy golf outing for WJR radio.

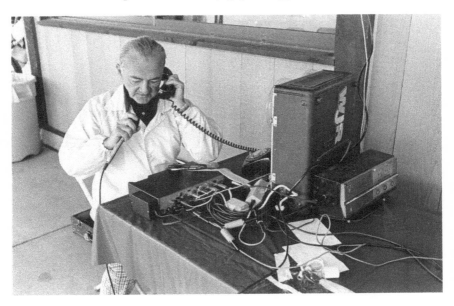

Working in the booth, listening and giving directions at the same time.

Harry Heilmann, the Announcer and the Salesman

Harry was the first Tiger announcer I worked for when I was hired in 1948. Back then baseball was a so-so sport with a small number of fans to cheer the players along. Year after year, they needed a person like Harry. He was funny and knew everything there was to know about baseball, and walked, talked, thought, acted, and rooted for the Detroit Tigers.

The purse strings around the radio business were small back in the late 1940s. We would air the home games live and the away games from the Telenews Theater located in Detroit's Grand Circus Park. We were in the basement lounge with glass windows separating the broadcasters from the assembled audience, just like a Hollywood studio. Sometimes as many as five hundred people were in the audience. Harry sat and looked out at the audience, and by his right elbow was the Western Union ticker tape machine. This is where we got the play-by-play information for the away game via Morey Hendry, the Western Union operator.

*The Telenews Theatre in Detroit where Harry Heilmann would broadcast
away games.*

Harry described the game smoothly, just like he was at the game. The tape read what the game was doing and also when there was a sensational play. He would see the information about three innings behind what he was announcing, so he would say, "Folks, I have a feeling that in St. Louis there will be a homer by Red Schoendienst." He told people he had a feeling all the time; his feeling came right from the ticker tape with the homer. Harry continued on with the game and then burst out with excitement, "Schoendienst hit a homer just like I thought he would!" The secret was the tickertape.

Harry was quite the salesman. He would barnstorm throughout the State of Michigan and talk all the radio stations into broadcasting the games live. He was so successful in getting the contracts that I counted forty-two new stations that year in Michigan, Ohio, Indiana, and Illinois. So wherever a fan went during the summer, they could hear Harry Heilmann and the Tigers on the radio.

Several years later, in Bradenton, Florida, Heilmann headed for home after the game. There weren't any roads where he was, not like today. So he took a ferryboat from Bradenton across the Tampa Bay, and he got sick from the rough waters. I had his suitcase with his commercials, so I took the roundabout way through Riverview, Florida, all on two lanes of blacktop (there was no I-4 then). When I got to the Lakeland Terrace Hotel to deliver the suitcase, Harry was sitting on the bed and wheezing. I called an ambulance and the hotel manager. He went to the hospital for treatment. He had a collapsed lung. That's when Ty Tyson and Paul Williams replaced Harry. I will never forget the good old days broadcasting Tiger baseball with Harry.

The Grapefruit League

Baseball games were different in the old days because spring training was different in the old days. Some cities did not have anything but a home and visitor dugout and a dressing room. In the early years, the Tigers would dress in their uniforms, and by the end of the day, they were pretty sweaty. Which meant if they had lost the game, they were mad. Lakeland's Henley Field Stadium didn't have seats for the fans, so everyone had to stand for the game. I set up my equipment on the roof of the dugout on a card table. Harry Heilmann and I would do the game in the hot sun only five feet from the players yelling off the field and the fans standing behind the dugout.

As part of the Grapefruit League in the early 1950s, we would travel all over Florida to play baseball. One game was scheduled in Tampa against Cincinnati; I remember our facility being in a circus barn. Our booth was in the stands over the entranceway for animals in the Tampa fairgrounds. Later, in the 1960s, we moved to Al Lopez Field to play Cincinnati, the same place where Raymond James Stadium stands now.

March 1967, setting up for a game in Lakeland, Florida.

We used to play the Yankees in West Palm Beach, and later at an airport complex with the signal tower ten feet behind us. About two miles northeast at Pompano Beach, the Washington Senators had spring training. About a half-hour drive to Miami was the spring home of the Baltimore Orioles, Miami Stadium. The location of the press box in Miami was two hundred feet high, above the third floor, right under the roof in a sling—a ten-foot-by-four-foot box attached to the facing.

My official pass to the best pressroom during spring training.

Paul Williams and Ty Tyson did the Detroit games from the sling booth. When it was Paul's turn to describe the play-by-play, it was just about hot dog time in the radio booth. Like the hatch on a submarine, an usher would hand down a bag of food. Imagine a microphone on a stand, Paul chomping on a hot dog and announcing the game. I would bet the audience never imagined what happened in the booth.

In the old days, we would broadcast from a sling booth. There was little room to move around in those days.

The Philadelphia Phillies played in Jack Russell Stadium in Clearwater, Florida, while the Toronto team played in Dunedin, Florida, which was only two miles north. Another group of teams close together were the Tigers in Lakeland, the Cincinnati Reds in Plant City, and the Cleveland Indians in Cypress Gardens, ten miles east of Lakeland. Kansas City played in Baseball City, Florida, the L.A. Dodgers in Vero Beach, and the New York Mets in Fort Pierce, all of which were in our neighborhood. Though the name and the place changed with each team as we traveled throughout the League, the game itself didn't, and we played ball as best we could every time.

At the time, other stadiums near Orlando had no motels. My family and I rented a room that looked like an Indian teepee, which cost us five bucks a night. Sarasota had a ballpark as good as Lakeland's park. The Red Sox trained there and one day Ted Williams got a fast pitch and fouled it into the netting. It went through the netting and hit my wife, June, on the shoulder. Ted yelled sorry and June waved back. Later, Sarasota hosted the St. Louis team (back then it was not uncommon for teams to switch locations for spring training) where Jack Buck and the screamer, Harry Caray, were the announcers. One day Buck came over to June and said he hit big at the track and handed June a one-hundred-dollar bill just because he was nice. A hundred dollars back then was a REALLY big deal.

Always well dressed for the games in the Grapefruit League.

Horror at Home Plate

Jerry Priddy, second baseman for the Detroit Tigers in the early 1950s, had the worst accident I ever witnessed in my fifty years of baseball. We were winning the game. Jerry was on base, and one of the guys hit a single so Jerry started running, looking back over his shoulder to see if the coast was clear to run. The next batter had stood up by the plate and raised his hand for the general signal *not* to slide into home. But Jerry missed the signal and kept coming in for the slide. His spikes had caught the plate and kept his foot in place, even as the rest of his body came after. His leg bone had been broken. The radio booth was located just above home plate and the third baseline. We were thirty feet away when it happened. When it was over, I looked towards Jerry's leg and his pant leg had been ripped and I could see the bleeding bone sticking out about four inches. I never forgot such a horrible sight at home plate.

Cooperstown

Van Patrick and I had a game scheduled for Cooperstown, New York, to play against the Dodgers. So Spike Briggs called Van and offered to fly the broadcast gang to the game. Spike owned an amphibious airplane, which he could put down on land or water, and that was how we got to Cooperstown. We got in the plane, which Spike called "The Duck."

It was about noon on a clear day when we flew from Detroit over the New York Finger Lakes and then onto the lake that borders the Hall of Fame Exhibit building in Cooperstown. The pilot ferried up to a little mooring walkway, tied the plane, and cut the motors. He opened the door to get out, and I was the first one out with my equipment trunk.

After grabbing the trunk, I stepped on the catwalk to the lawn. On my first step off "The Duck," I set the microphones down and looked up to the big glass window of the Exhibition Hall. I waved my hands in a welcoming gesture and saw an awesome sight: thirty-five Baseball Hall of Famers were standing on the patio and waving back. What a thrill! There had been a special event that weekend at the Baseball Hall of Fame, with many of these great players in attendance. We aired the game and flew "The Duck" back home. Seeing those Hall of Famers waving at me was one of the biggest thrills of my entire life.

Van Patrick, a great announcer and a good friend.

Don't Challenge the Boss

We were in Bradenton playing the Pittsburgh Pirates. We had a rickety grandstand and no pressroom. Bob Prince and Nelly King were the local broadcasters, and they were doing a good job for KDKA. I had received a call from Kenny Kimball to do the Pittsburgh game on KDKA, and when the game started there were three men in the booth: Prince, Nelly, and me. We were working when suddenly the back door came open in the second inning, and we could hear loud voices coming in because about a half-dozen agency men were getting loud. These agency men were the men who handled all the money, the ones who paid the bills and the ones who signed the paychecks. Prince had a tough time broadcasting, and all of a sudden he yelled for me to turn off all the mikes except for the microphone on the field. Prince then chased all the loudmouth drunks out of the booth, and we finished the game. The next day, Nelly King did the whole game by himself. He said that Prince had been fired because he had chased the bosses out of the booth. So you see, not everyone gets away with everything all the time.

Engineers Save the Day

The location of the radio booth in the Cleveland Indian's stadium was also a hanging sling off the facing of the second deck. It was near home plate, out in the open, and exposed to the elements. We were in one of two slings, one for the home team broadcasters and one for the visiting crew. Our seating arrangement in the first booth was Mel Ott, Van Patrick, Ray Quaid (director for television), and me; we were all within arm's length of the home booth. The arrangement next to me was the Cleveland engineer, Fergeson, then Hank Greenberg (part owner and general manager for Cleveland), and their announcer, Dudley. When it started to rain, it came lightly and I had time to cover my amplifier with a newspaper, but Fergeson did not cover his. I looked over and saw a big puff of smoke coming out of his amplifier. His amp was toast, so I immediately got out my spare amplifier and handed it over to Fergy. All we had to do was disconnect the AC plug, two microphones, and the broadcast phone loop, which took about twenty-five seconds. He then hooked up my amplifier and plugged in the two microphones, AC cord, and phone lines. It took him about a minute to change things and amazingly the studio saw the drop-off. They went to a one-and-a-half-minute commercial, and when the spot was over, Fergy was on the air again and nothing had been lost. Hank was so amazed at how the engineers saved the day! He was ready and waiting to be interviewed, we never missed a beat, and the Cleveland fans were pleased.

Mel Ott, Van Patrick, Ray Quaid, and I in Cleveland, Ohio before a game.

Florida Crabs

Back in the late 1950s and early 1960s many roads on the way down to Florida were not like the interstates we have now, but rather two-lane blacktops. Often, my wife, June, drove down to Florida without me because I had to travel with the team, but I never worried about her because she was a very good driver. When we had a game in a big Florida city, June and Linda would go shopping (one of their favorite hobbies, even today) while I was busy working the game.

The ballgames during spring training were mostly transmitted to Michigan on the weekends, so during the week, I got to spend lots of time with my family, which I loved to do. Even though the Tigers played in Lakeland, our favorite place to stay was on Siesta Key near Sarasota, Florida.

One year we took June's mother and a friend of Linda's with us to Siesta Key, and it was a blast. We rented a small home that was up on stilts (in case of a hurricane) right on the beach, and, of course, houses back then did not have air conditioning. June was a serious sun worshiper and loved the beach. At night the two kids and I spent time looking for blue crabs. The girls were scared of the crabs, so I would set one of the girls on my left shoulder and one of the girls on my right shoulder and head for the sand bar out about two hundred feet from shore. We would watch the crabs scurry under us, and the kids would scream as loud as they could. I think I can still hear the ringing in my ears. We used flashlights in the dark and spotted more crabs when we got back to the sand on the beach.

My beautiful wife June, sunbathing in the Florida sun.

We also loved to walk the shell line and pick up hundreds of sand dollars, sharks teeth, and shells of every kind. But we also knew not to step on or go near the man-o-war squid. They had poison in every tentacle. Some years in Florida the beach was full of dead fish from the Red Tide, which was not good for shelling or swimming.

One time, on the way home from spring training, I remember a tornado passed through Georgia as we were driving. We could see it coming, but it was far ahead of us. When we got to the road where the tornado had hit, there were electrical wires over the road. June said to stop, but I did not listen to her, as usual, and stepped on the gas. The car jumped, and without even a spark, we made it past and lived to tell the story. Driving back then was always an adventure.

Grand Ole Opry

One year, at the end of the spring-training schedule in Florida, on the way back to Michigan, the Tigers would pick a team, and both teams would play an exhibition game. Some of the cities we played in included Ashville, Knoxville, Nashville, Birmingham, Cincinnati, Washington, and Atlanta. These games were played before the regular season opener. Sometimes I had to ride on the plane with the team, and June would take Linda and the car and meet us at the exhibition game.

One time, the Tigers and Cincinnati Reds were playing in Nashville. Joe Nuxhall and Marty Brennaman invited June and me to the Grand Ole Opry. We sat on stage and saw everything from behind the curtain. We were within a few feet of the stars. Minnie Pearl, Roy Acuff, Jimmy Dickins, and the biggies were all there, and we had a great time at the Grand Ole Opry. I never did get to see my favorite of all time, Hank Williams, though. We stayed on the stage in the background for two shows, and it was a night I will never forget.

Flying Rules!

I never knew what to expect when flying. When we would fly from L.A. to Seattle, the pilots made sure to announce where we were, like over the lava flats in the mountains of California. There was one volcano hole, I remember, filled with water, and the pilot told us that a bomber was down in the pit, the hole was miles deep, and nobody could ever go that deep. So they are still down there, just like the battle ships (or wagons to us sailors) at Pearl Harbor, which means that the guys will never come up.

It was on one of those Seattle trips that we played ball in a stadium called Sicks Stadium, where the Seattle Pilots played. That was because the owner's name was Mr. Emil Sick. That ball game was a boring one, so my eyes scanned the horizon and I saw snow covering the top half of Mt. Rainier. It was a beautiful sight.

When we played a series in Seattle, all the pilots would go out of their way to get as close to the snow line as possible so we could see the deer, goats, and other animals. We broke the flying rules, but nobody ever reported it. Eventually, the Seattle Pilots became the Milwaukee Brewers.

For these flights, the seating on the charter planes was not strict, but there was a system to it. The first seats after the small kitchen on the plane were almost always the same for each trip. The card players and the cribbage gang were always in the rear. In the middle, over the wings, were the coaches, writers, and office gang. Now, Norman Cash and Billy Martin always occupied the front seats, and the second row was for Ernie Harwell, who always wanted the window seat, and me. On the third row was Willie Horton and Gates Brown. When it was mealtime on the flight, we had meat, potatoes and gravy, a small salad, and pecan pie. Here's the good part: since Ernie and I were served almost first, we gobbled it all up before all the other guys had their trays. Since I was familiar with the players' habits, I knew who ate what. Willie never ate his pecan pie and was a slow eater. So I'd put my hand on the headrest of my seat, and low and behold, Willie would put his pie in it because he knew I was a pie beggar. It always worked. I used to go up and down the aisle and grab all the pies before the flight attendants could get to them and throw them in the garbage. On some flights I'd eat ten to fifteen pecan pies.

There was this other flight from Cleveland to Detroit where we had lost the game and everyone seemed grumpy. This became a problem at mealtime. The players discussed what they wanted with the stewardesses, and it took too long; we had only eighteen minutes airtime for the flight. So Charley Creedon, the Tigers' traveling secretary, called the gals to sit down and he said, "Howard, feed these guys." Now, nobody was going to argue with the radio engineer, and I took advantage of the situation. I grabbed the whole tray of sandwiches, passed them out, nobody griped, and all went well, even when Charley also limited the gang to one drink per flight. We did all this within the eighteen minutes. From wheels up in Cleveland to wheels down in Detroit, I satisfied all of the players and everybody was happy. Charley Creedon shook my hand—what a thrill. He was the nicest guy on the plane well next to Ernie, of course.

We had our exciting moments on flights to and from Detroit. One time a goose flew into the outboard portside engine. The captain came on the intercom and told us not to worry, that we'd just use the three engines, and, if needed, he could fly the plane with only one engine. Another time out of Los Angeles, we had to fly west over the Pacific to gain elevation and fly east to pass over the high Mojave range of mountains. As we flew along, another plane was on a landing pattern and heading straight for us. Quickly, our pilot took a nosedive, and the other plane climbed up and out of the way. During the nosedive, Ernie was in the aisle about to go to his seat, and as I looked over, I saw his feet lift about a foot off the floor, pitter-pattering until we leveled off. Willie Horton was sitting two seats behind me, and he was so scared on the nosedive that he grabbed the headrest of the seat in front of him and tore it off. That guy was strong!

Another time we had the jitters was when we hit bad weather leaving for Baltimore after a night game in Detroit. The captain got on the intercom and said, "Fellows, Baltimore is socked in and Detroit is socked in, so we cannot go back." The only place with a hole in the clouds that was open was Harrisburg, Pennsylvania. We circled for an hour and a half, with lightning in all directions. Some of the players thought we would never make it, but then WPCU Baltimore tower said, "Come on in," and we landed safely.

On another flight to Seattle, we were going against a high-altitude wind and had to use more fuel than expected. Our charter captain told us that we were going to land in Salt Lake City to refuel. Just east of this city is the Wasatch, a mountain range in the Rockies, and as we were passing these mountains, I looked out and had never seen the world so far away. During the flight, Ernie, George Kell, and I sat on the portside of the plane, just over the wing. The flight attendant brought our meal at the right time, and all went well. On the food tray was a glass of champagne for each one of us. I downed mine and Ernie took just a sip of his, and then passed it to me. "Thanks, Ern." I gulped it. Kell did the same—one sip and he slipped his drink onto my tray. The flight attendant didn't know that I had drank three glasses of champagne, so she refilled them all again and I did the same thing. I ended up drinking nine champagnes on one flight! No wonder I couldn't see straight. When we landed, everyone got off the plane, and Jordan, the pilot, took the plane to the gas pump. I guess Ernie and Kell took me through the terminal, where I think I remember buying some post cards to send back home to my mom and sister.

Our next flight was to New York City, and that's only about one hour away from Fleetwood, Pennsylvania—my hometown. I had the day off in New York City and got a ride home to Pennsylvania. When I arrived home, my sister, Arlene, showed me a postcard from Salt Lake City with a small bag of salt glued to it. She thanked me for it. I still remember my mother's face when I saw her, though I didn't have the heart to tell her and my sister that I was plastered when I sent it. They just wouldn't understand what happens when a young boy leaves home and goes along with Tiger ballplayers.

*Front row: Gates Brown, Dick McAuliffe, George Kell, Bill Freehan,
Phil Regan, Al Kaline, Don Mossi, Bob Swift, Bud Jordan, Charlie Dressen,
Charlie Creedon, Pat Mullin, Stubby Overmeir, Wayne Blackburn, Frank Lary,
George Smith, Bill Faul.*

*Back row: Rocky Colovito, Gus Triandos, Bill Bruton, Phil Regan, Terry Fox,
Mickey Lolich, Don Wert, Fred Gladding, Mike Rourke, George Thomas,
Norm Cash, Jim Bunning, Whitey Herzog, Ronnie Kline, F. Sullivan, me,
Watson Spolstra, Jack Homel*

Lightning Strikes

In the early 1960s, we had a game in Baltimore. The Orioles finished the game through nine innings, and the Tigers won. At the very end of the game, the players ran for cover in the dugout and the dressing room, as it was beginning to storm. The game was just ending when lightning struck and torrents of rain fell. Meanwhile, I was with the radio announcers in the booth, which in Baltimore was equipped with a tarp instead of glass windows. Van Patrick was introducing the post-game recap when the lightning got closer. It was so loud and long we had the microphones open to let Detroit WKMH hear the noise. After the broadcast, we let the tarp down to prevent the rain from getting everyone wet. As usual, I was watching the vacated field, and there was water all over it. All of a sudden a lightning bolt hit inside the stadium. Typically, the left fielder had a spot where he spent the majority of the game, a place where the grass was usually trampled bare, and it was at that exact spot I saw the lighting strike. It blew smoke and burned the ground. If this happened during the game, the left fielder would have been toast. It is amazing the difference a couple of minutes can make. Van Patrick ended the post-game so quickly that I think he missed two commercials. But, so it goes.

Food, My Favorite Part of the Job

The secret to my radio engineering success was simple. I entered the broadcast booth and set up the WPA amplifier and the three microphones as the crowd picked up. One team was just like the other. Or I should say all the teams do exactly the same in the eyes of the engineer. The game goes first inning and break, second inning and break, third inning and break, and so on. As the man with the ears and the stopwatch, all I had to do was open the microphone and give the reporter the go signal. There was always a break in the action every half inning from beginning to end of the game. So the process was simple. Start the announcers and stop the announcers, and I treated them all alike. I would show no mercy. I told the big-shot announcer to shut up and they did. So when it was time to talk, I would stand by and they had to shut up until I told them to talk.

Now, about the food, the Dodgers had the most fabulous press lounge of all the teams. They had waitresses and busboys by the dozen, and their food was first class all the way. They had ice cream, steak, and hotdogs. When we would get done with our first course, the waitresses would insist on ice cream sundaes—and, of course, I would have to have one after the first round.

In my opinion, Cleveland's home press box room was second in the league. They had all the goodies. You could have paid fifty bucks at a restaurant for the kind of food they served. They had good side dishes, and we did an equally good job of gobbling them up. In Cleveland the Emil Bozzard family, the grounds crew in charge of field maintenance, were welcome to have lunch there every game day. They would sit around and make small talk with us before they went back on the field.

The pressroom in Yankee Stadium was the biggest flop in the circuit. Even during spring training at Legend's Field the food was terrible, and we had to pay six bucks per day.

Some of the stadiums of the American League didn't impress me too much, so we didn't eat there too often. I would rather eat with Van Patrick, Vince Desmond, or Charlie Creedon because they were the bankers on the club, and they would buy me dinner.

In the early 1950s, there wasn't a pressroom in Washington, so we would buy hotdogs and take them into the radio booth on top of the grandstand. Broadcasting for WTOP was Arch McDonald, who also advertised for Wheaties, the breakfast of champions. In the press box, "Wheatville Arch" was only five foot four inches tall, weighed over two hundred pounds, and was a nice fellow at all times.

As for Lakeland, they used to serve only hotdogs, but as the years went by, they eventually set up a temporary tent to serve the press and radio crew before the game. The food there was excellent, and during the game, they had a tray of goodies in case you got hungry again. Besides that they had a refrigerator and served popsicles, ice cream sandwiches, and all small frozen snacks. I knew when we had a one-minute-forty-five-second commercial at WJR, so I would turn off the microphone and grab a handful of goodies for Ernie and Paul. Now here is a secret I can tell about Ernie: he would accept a frozen popsicle but would only nibble about the corner and then pass it back to me. I thought Ernie was the greatest. I often brought donuts to the booth, and again, Ernie would only take a bite and I got to eat the rest. I sure miss the goodies at the ballpark and all the fellows around the press box. Excuse me for a minute; I'm going for a donut.

Ernie always enjoyed a good meal at the ballpark.

See my big smile, I loved the food at the ballpark too!

King of the Rain Delay

The engineer had odd duties sometimes, like when the team was in a rain delay. The reporters would go for a hot dog or something, and I would open my information microphone on a closed circuit. I'd tell the forty-two stations not to put me on the air due to the hold. That was typically against the rules, but I was king of the rain delay. I would tell them how bad the storm was and when it was getting better or worse, and if we went back on the air again, I would forewarn all the stations to stand by because in one minute my stop watch would indicate that all hands were ready. This way it always went smoothly. Everything in the broadcast empire went according to rules, and nobody strayed. There were times when the storms would last for over an hour, and to keep all the net control rules from going to sleep, I'd tell the forty-two networks how bad the field was under water. Sometimes I'd tell all the guys, especially in the upper peninsula, how many beautiful girls were at the game, which gave the networks notice never to put the engineer's voice on the air. One disc jockey in Kalamazoo, Otis Bucannan, listened to me for years. He would look forward to a rain delay, and while his station played music on the air, he would listen to me on the closed circuit. When Bucannan came to work in Detroit, he said he wanted to meet me in person and tell me how he liked the closed circuit as much as the ball game.

Rain or shine, I always loved my job.

A Storm Approaching

Just about ten miles from Lakeland, Florida, are the cities of Winter Haven and Cypress Gardens. The Cleveland Indians' stadium was one hundred yards from the lake and was called Land-O-Lakes Stadium. The press box was just five feet from the last row of paying customers. They could hear us and we could hear them, and sometimes it was hard to keep them quiet so we could broadcast the game. The old-timer announcers were Jimmy Dudley and Bob Neal, who really didn't like each other, so they sat with one chair in between them and would always argue off the air. They also had a radio engineer from WWE, Dick Saterweit, and before that was Jim Shroedel and Harry Dennis. There were times when the engineer had to sit between Jim Shroeder and Harry Dennis to keep them talking baseball; otherwise they had differing opinions.

One day at about nine a.m., storms approached, and by noon the rain and lightning was all around. My equipment was set up and ready to go about half an hour before the game. The lightning struck so close to the booth that I saw the corona (smoke from lightning) coming from my burned up amplifier. It knocked it dead as a doornail, and the engineers at WJR were telling me to use another phone line. We argued, WJR and me, until ten minutes before airtime. Then the PA popped up and said the game was called because water covered the field. That is the closest I ever came to being electrocuted. For the next game, we went to Jacksonville, and I used a spare amplifier and saved the day. To this day, I still shudder from the thought of using that amplifier with lightening dancing all around me. There would have been no more Howard Stitzel!

A Game Called on Account of Rain by MISTAKE!

The night sky was cloudy and threatening at Tiger Stadium. It was 1971, and we were in the late innings when the rain started. It poured and poured, and eventually the umpires stopped the game. So we sat there in the radio booth and did nothing. After about an hour of sitting around, we heard the squawk box, which is an intercom to talk between the press box and radio both. Now, this was an antiquated style of squawk box, but that's what was there, between the radio booth and press box on the third floor, where Hal Middlesworth was located. He was the official announcer upstairs who relayed all-important directions to the stadium. Ernie, Ray Lane, and I were really close to the squawk box, and we heard Hal say that the game was called and we would have a doubleheader tomorrow. So back on the microphones, I warned the radio stations on the network that we had news and would resume the broadcast in one minute. I started my stopwatch and we went on the air again. Ernie announced that the game was canceled and we would have a doubleheader tomorrow. So he quickly signed off and rushed down to his car and left the parking lot. In the meantime, Billy Martin was listening to the broadcast and came out of the clubhouse, and on the top step of the dugout he yelled up at me and Ray to say the game had not been called. Ray was in a dither and had to call the correct information. Ernie was at the intersection of Grand River and Trumbull and was listening to the radio when he heard the game had not been cancelled. Ernie immediately made a U-turn to come back at the booth. He found out that the message from Hal Middlesworth on the bum squawk box was missing a word. The message should have been "*If*" the game is called. So we finished the game and all went home.

The very next day the roof fell in. Jim Campbell called Hal, Ernie, Ray, and me into the office and was steaming. He had hit the roof. He said he had to reimburse all that money from the ticket sales for that game. Ernie explained that we missed the "If" and all three of us heard it the same. As he scolded us, I stood up and said that my ears were only one foot away from the speaker, and yes, we missed the "If." At that point, Jim had had enough and he popped up and said Howard keep your mouth shut. I guess he would have fired the best gang out there, but he knew he would never get replacements that were good as we were. So life went on, and we were still employees.

In 1967, Ernie Harwell, Ray Lane, and I sharing some fun times in Lakeland, Florida.

In 1968, Ernie Harwell, Ray Lane, and I continued our fun times in the radio booth. Notice the tickertape on the floor? That was what we used for information before computers.

My Friend, Ernie Harwell

A great voice and great broadcaster for sports, Ernie Harwell came to the Tigers from Baltimore. He replaced Van Patrick when there was a sponsor change from Goebel Beer to Stroh's Brewing Company in the late 1950s. Van Patrick was replaced after the sponsor change because of his close association with Goebel Beer and their longtime mascot, a bantam, named Brewster Rooster.

Ernie had a secret in the broadcast booth that was not well known. He was so diligent that every day or so he would update a series of index cards (before computers, of course) with player statistics and would reference them when a critical or simple question arose while calling the game. That way he was never wrong.

My typical view of Ernie in the booth, calling the plays of the game.

He was sincere when he was working the microphone, but sometimes he would slip and go along with one of my jokes that we would pull between an engineer and the two stars in the booth. One day I was tired of reading the Western Union ticker tape machine, so I made up my own announcement. Ray was on the air, and it was Ernie's three-inning rest. It was a day with nothing happening on the field just below our booth, so I wrote a note and told Ernie not to spill the beans to Ray about the joke coming up. He read it, turned away, and gave the note to Ray, who read it just like many announcements that came from the mail we got. The note read: "Ladies and gents, we have a special announcement to make." Then all was quiet in the booth and Ray read on the air: "Enal Yar is with us today and he's celebrating his ninety-ninth birthday!" He was actually saying Ray Lane backwards. Ernie couldn't hold his breath any longer and started to laugh right into the microphone on the air. Ray was wondering what was going on. Ernie said, "Read that last announcement again," and Ray did. We had Ray read it again, and a minute later Ray figured it out, got mad at us for a second, and then started belly laughing. We all had a good joke on Ray, who was such a great sport.

Ernie and I in our later years.

While Ernie and Ray are busy calling the game, I have time to wave to the camera.

Sharing another smile with my friend, Ernie.

One of the most famous pictures of the early 1960's.
The picture is still hanging at the new Comerica Park.
Courtesy of the Ernie Harwell Sports Collection, Detroit Public Library.

The famous picture again on the ticket of one of the last games ever played at Tiger Stadium in 1999.

Lineup of Famous and Infamous Baseball Legends

During the many years working with the Tigers in various ball fields and with so many players and other radio personalities, I have been blessed to meet and know so many people. I can remember their faces and names and their stories like it was yesterday. I have seen the lineup change, and as Robert Duvall says to Robert Redford in the great baseball movie *The Natural*, "They come and they go, Hobbs. They come and they go."

Paul Howard "Dizzy" Trout (Tiger pitcher, 1939–52, and Tiger announcer, 1953–55)

Dizzy was a rookie in the booth and had his own way of describing a ball game. He would watch the third base coach signal to home plate and to the men on base. If the players didn't get the coach's sign, Dizzy would give out a loud whistle, so loud the people in the stands could hear, and so could the third base coach. Then the coach knew to repeat the sign. Now poor Van Patrick would cover his ears and my amplifier needle would go crazy when Dizzy would whistle.

One day in New York as we were broadcasting, a foul ball came at us at a hundred miles per hour. Dizzy tried to catch the ball, but it bounced off his finger, hit the tabletop, and he wound up with a broken knuckle. But Dizzy still never shied away from a good catch.

Back in the Detroit booth, Dizzy would contradict calls that Van Patrick would make, and oftentimes they would argue. However, Dizzy was usually right about the call. We found out later that Dizzy was deaf in his left ear, the ear closest to Van.

One day, after hearing them argue again, I muted the microphones and told them, "Let's do the game now." We all shook hands and understood one another better. There was one deaf broadcaster and one happy engineer. I was king of the booth again.

Virgil Trucks (Tiger pitcher, 1941–52)

In the old days, the team traveled on a single-track train. On August 25, 1952, Virgil had a no-hitter against the New York Yankees. Previously that same year, on May 15, Virgil also had a no-hitter against the Washington Senators. After that second no-hitter in the same year, three radio shows called Trucks to be on the air. They wanted to pay him a thousand dollars for each interview. Of all things, he refused and said, "I would rather have fun with the guys on the overnight train ride to Boston." To this day, Virgil is one of only three pitchers to throw two no-hitters in one season.

Billy Hitchcock (Tiger infielder, 1942, 1946, 1953)

Billy lived in a rental home in Lincoln Park, Michigan, and he did not own a car so he would ride to the games with me. All the way home, he would be a nervous wreck and often say, "Howard, you drive too fast." I tended to do that.

Bob Swift (Tiger catcher, 1944–53, and coach, 1965)

Bob was a great guy and was as tough as they come. He always fought hard to win the game. Known as "Swifty," Bob came back as a Tiger coach when manager Chuck Dressen had a heart attack during spring training.

George Kell (Tiger third baseman, 1946–52, and Tiger announcer, 1959–63)

George, Larry Sherry, and Earl Torgeson loved to play bridge. On one trip, they needed a fourth player. After I set up for the broadcast, there was some time to kill so they asked me to join them. This only lasted one game. All three of them said I talked too much, and they kicked me out of the bridge game.

George was a great player and was part of the nicest pair in broadcasting, Kell and Kaline.

Burt Bell (NFL commissioner, 1946–59)

Burt used to have a car waiting for Van Patrick and me when we visited Philadelphia. We would often drive over to the boardwalk in Atlantic City. Burt was a baseball fan even though he ran the football league. Burt and Van were good friends. I always appreciated his generosity.

Pat "PJ" Mullin (Tiger outfielder, 1946–53)

PJ was always very friendly to me, loved to talk, and was also from Pennsylvania.

Vic Wertz (Tiger right fielder, 1947–52)

Vic would stand on the top step of the dugout during the national anthem. When he took his hat off, his bald head would shine brightly in the sun, causing many broadcasters to laugh. Vic was a very big guy, and after his baseball career, he became a distributor for Goebel Beer.

Sonny Eliot (Detroit Weatherman, 1947–2010)

Sonny was the great weatherman in Detroit. He loved sports, especially the Tigers. He would sit with us in the broadcast booth during many of the games if he was not doing the weather forecast for Channel 2, and later for Channel 4. He was a star all around the ballpark, no matter where he sat; however, his favorite spot was in the booth with us. Sonny loved the booth because he loved the action.

Bud Lynch, Sonny Elliot and I at a Red Wings game in Detroit.

Joe Ginsberg (Tiger catcher, 1948, 1950–53)

Joe was a really good catcher and poker player. Joe was the catcher when Virgil Trucks pitched his no-hitter. During our long flights across the county, Joe and Van would play poker for hours. Joe would always win.

Teddy Lyons (Tiger manager, 1949–52)

Prior to coming to Detroit, Teddy was a pitcher for the Chicago White Sox. A south-sider from Chicago, he knew all the good and bad people in Chicago. When we would ride to Sox ballpark from the Hotel del Prado, Teddy pointed his fingers outside the bus to indicate where Al Capone lived and showed us the garage where the Valentine massacre happened. Teddy was always our Chicago tour guide.

Marlin Stuart (Tiger pitcher, 1949–52)

Marlin was from Arkansas and was one of the nicest guys on the team. Before his baseball career, he was a poor farmer, as most farmers were back then, except for George Kell. Kell had a ranch outside of Swiftin, Arkansas, and would take his Jeep to check on his back forty acres and all his cows and bulls. Marlin was envious of George and nicknamed him the "windshield farmer." They were good friends and loved joking around with one another.

Van Patrick (Tiger announcer, 1949, 1952–59)

After a game in Kansas City, the bus for the players left, and because Van had post-games shows that took too long, I missed the bus. He felt bad and he yelled to me, "I'll treat you to dinner tonight." So we packed up our equipment and hailed a cab to the best rib joint in town. As we were enjoying the best ribs we'd ever had, out of the main entrance came the biggest person I had ever seen: "Wilt the Stilt" Chamberlain, the basketball star. He passed by and the people begged for his autograph, but it wasn't their night. One boy ran up to Chamberlain and asked for his autograph. Wilt put his hand on the boy's head, pushed him back, and the boy fell on his rump. The whole restaurant saw what happened, and Van immediately stood up to challenge the seven one, 275-pound basketball star. I got up and stopped Van. I told Van to sit down, and he listened to me and we finished our ribs. Wouldn't you know it, Van even finished a second rack of ribs after the debacle. I can tell you, I saved my King, and to this day, Van will always be King to me.

Another time, Van and I were in the booth at Comiskey Park. There was a stadium pole situated right in front of the booth blocking the view of right field. During the game, a fly ball headed to the right field. Van kept saying it was caught, but he really couldn't see where the ball was headed. I pushed him from behind so that he could see where the ball was going. It was not caught, and Van quickly and smoothly talked his way out. He said, "Wait a minute folks, he's juggling the ball and now he lost it." And the old smoothie got out of that one. Van could do anything on the radio since no one could watch baseball on television back then.

Mel Ott, Van Patrick, and Bill Veck at Tiger Stadium.

Freddy Hutchinson (Tiger pitcher, 1949, and manager, 1952–54)

Freddy was a great and passionate pitcher. When the manager, Red Rolfe (1949–52), pulled Freddy out of the game, Freddy would hit, with his bare fists, all of the light bulbs down the hallway from the bench to the dressing room. John Hand, the clubhouse manager, would wrap up his hands and put ointment on his wounds and not let anyone into the clubhouse until Freddy cooled down. Then Freddy became the Tiger manager when Red was fired in 1952.

Bud Lynch (Detroit Red Wings Public Address Announcer, 1950–2012)

Bud was the first television broadcaster for the Detroit Red Wings back in the early 1950s. Because this was the first time an announcer did a hockey game on live TV, there really was no good space to do the broadcast at the Olympia, so the organization built a booth using Bud's specifications. After it was complete, there was a big flaw. When Bud sat down he could not see the hockey rink on the west side, which was opposite the booth. To do a good job, he had to bend down to describe the game, and he grumbled all the time. When I worked at the Olympia with Al Nagler, he suggested we trade booths so that Bud would have a better view of the rink. However, management did not approve the move, but I had the answer to the problem: the next home game, I nailed some boards together, stole my wife's bathroom mirrors and built a submarine periscope about four feet long. Bud was thrilled because he could now see everything! That made Bud Lynch happy, and I saved the day.

Dick Bartell (Tiger coach, early 1950s)

Dick's duties were to keep the clubhouse operational, which included being the keeper of the baseball bag. He had to ensure the balls were well scuffed for the game, no new white balls made it to the field. Many times, I would go to Dick and ask him for a dirty baseball, but he'd always refuse. Instead, he would give me three brand new ones. Because of Dick's generosity, all the kids in Southgate had new baseballs to play with.

Charlie "King Kong" Keller (Tiger outfielder, 1950–51)

Charlie got the nickname, King Kong, because of his strength. He was short, stocky, and had hair all over his body. He never liked that nickname much, so I never called him King Kong. Instead, when he was in Detroit we called him the "Detroit Bear."

Ray Herbert (Tiger pitcher, 1950–54)

Ray was a talented pitcher but not a fast runner. After we traded him to Kansas City, he eventually became an excellent pitcher. In 1962, as a pitcher for the White Sox, he won twenty games.

Billy Hoeft (Tiger pitcher, 1952–59)

The early 1950s were the fun years. I remember palling around with Billy in New York. We were on the subway to Coney Island when we heard some girls saying, "That's Billy Hoeft, the pitcher that beat the Yankees this afternoon." Billy then had a big smile on his face and felt like a million bucks.

Harvey Kuehn (Tiger shortstop, 1952–59)

Harvey was a good guy and won the American League batting crown in 1959. Eventually, he was traded to the Cleveland Indians for Rocky Colavito. Harvey lost his left leg because of a blood clot, but he returned to coaching just six months later. He managed the Milwaukee Brewers to their only World Series appearance.

Frank Lary, me, and Harvey Kuenn in the dugout before a game.

Fred Hatfield (Tiger third baseman, 1952–56)

Fred had an excellent throwing arm. He was always entertaining, happy, and fun to be around. We would call him "Scrap Iron."

Bill Tuttle (Tiger center fielder, 1952–57)

Bill played in center field and would often have to stand in water because the drain was clogged. You could see him running for a fly ball and splashing all the way. I wanted Van Patrick to talk about the field conditions and say: "Bill Tuttle in the puddle," but he never did.

Bill chewed lots of tobacco and unfortunately passed away from cancer. He became a volunteer for the National Spit Tobacco Education Program to raise awareness of the dangers of using chewing tobacco.

Matt Batts (Tiger catcher, 1952–54)

In the Shoreham Hotel in Washington, D.C., Matt would wait for me in the morning and scold me for being late. He said he was hungry and broke and wanted to use my expense account. "Let's get some eggs and toast," he would say. Matt was a funny fellow.

One time in Philadelphia, a ball was hit straight up into the sky. Matt had to twist his body so fast and so hard that he got a hernia. He stayed in a Philadelphia hospital until he was healthy enough to travel. We picked him up on our next game with Philadelphia. He resumed catching after healing quickly.

Al Kaline (Tiger right fielder, 1953–74, and announcer, 1975–2002)

Al came to the Detroit Tigers right out of high school. We called him "Izzy" because the Tigers couldn't determine "Izzy" a right fielder or "Izzy" or left fielder at the beginning of his career.

Kaline Corner was a part of the stands in right field at the old Tiger Stadium on Michigan and Trumbull. The stands were in the way whenever Al would catch a fly ball. The Tigers had to take that part of the stadium out so that he would not hurt himself. Kaline Corner is also a part of the new Comerica Park, where the Tigers now play.

One time, Al caught a fly ball at Yankee Stadium. When he got back to the dug out, he fainted, fell, and broke his arm. He missed the first two months of the famous 1968 season.

Al was the nicest Detroit Tiger. He was always friendly to his fans, especially kids, the press, and the radio crew. He never got mad at anyone and always gave interviews when asked. The best thing about Al was that he never refused an autograph. When I got into the booth, sometimes I had two, three, or even four baseballs. He would always sign them and then chase me out of the television booth. Don't forget his partner, George Kell, who was also nice to all of his fans.

Al Kaline at batting practice during a 1980's reunion of the 1968 World Series team.
Photograph courtesy of Rodney J. Turman.

Al and I sharing some laughs while I also get his autograph.
Photograph courtesy of Rodney J. Turman.

Ray Boone (Tiger infielder, 1953–59)

Ray had calcium on his knees and got shots of cortisone when needed. The shots would cure his knees for about three days. Dr. Livingood, the team doctor, used a needle on Boone that I swear was six inches long. Dr. Livingood also helped me the only time I didn't feel good when we were traveling. He gave me some medicine for a stomachache, and I felt better in no time.

Johnny Bucha (Tiger catcher, 1953)

Johnny was known to be the whistler behind the plate who gave his signal to the pitcher via a whistle sequence. When we would have a day off in New York, Johnny and I would hitchhike to Allentown, Pennsylvania, where he lived, and I would visit my mom and dad on the farm in Fleetwood, Pennsylvania.

Bob "Burly" Nieman (Tiger outfielder, 1953–54)

Once on a train trip to St. Louis, we both took our wives. Our wives talked the entire trip. This was the last trip we took our wives with us.

Red Wilson (Tiger catcher, 1954–60)

Red was #10 (all catchers wore the #10 back then). He was one of the nicest guys on the team; he was friendly and never argued with anyone. Red could cut all of the runners down at home plate or pick them off at first base. He had a hot arm.

Chick King (Tiger left fielder, 1954)

Chick was a big, strong guy with a great arm. He could throw directly to home plate from left field to get the runner out.

Jim Bunning (Tiger pitcher, 1955–63)

Jim threw low, hard pitches, which would make his hat fly off, and he would always get the batter out. Jim had a no-hitter in Boston in

1958. He was one of the best pitchers we had and always gave his best effort.

When things were not so lucrative in the 1960s, two players were assigned to the same room to save the organization some money. Jim and Rocky Colavito were roommates on the away games. The press and radio crews did not have to bunk together; we paid for our own lodging, meals, and air using a Campbell Ewald Advertisement Agency expense account. They were the only ones making money at the time.

July 1958, Jim Bunning and I posing for the camera before we begin our travels.

Mel Ott (Tiger announcer, 1956–58)

If you are an old-timer, you will remember the "King of Swat," Mel Ott from the New York Giants. He didn't play for the Tigers but joined us in the 1950s as an announcer.

During his first game at spring training in 1956, Mel was the new face on the scene. We set him up at the microphone and went through the opening process. As normal, I yelled, "Stand by," and gave him the motion to begin speaking. He started to say hello, and I noticed a new language in the booth, a southern drawl. I just had to let him know something, so I cut the microphone for a few seconds. I told him to speak English, and he looked at me with astonishment. Then, he began again and it all turned out all right. I was ordering the "King of Swat" around like I was the boss of the booth. From that time on, we were friends forever. Just think of this, a broadcast engineer telling the King how to talk; it still gives me chills.

Sadly, Mel died in an automobile accident in New Orleans in 1958.

Mel Ott, the King of Swat, up at bat.

Charley Maxwell (Tiger left fielder, 1956–60)

Charley's nickname was the "Sunday Performer," and fans considered him their hometown boy from PawPaw, Michigan. He got the nickname because he always hit a homerun on Sundays. The manager assigned him as a relief batter on Sundays because they knew they could count on him for at least one run every Sunday.

Charley rented a home in Taylor, Michigan, having me pick him up for games so he wouldn't have to drive to the ballpark. We would meet at the corner of Telegraph and Wick Roads and head to work together. It was always fun to ride home with him on Sundays.

Bobo Osborne (Tiger first baseman, 1957–59, 1961–62)

Bobo was a reasonable hitter with a big stature. At the end of the each ball game, he would enjoy a bottle of Goebel beer, brought to the team every week as a gift, and sit in the clubhouse until he was finished. John Hand, the clubhouse manager, would wait until he was finished to lock up.

Hank Aguirre (Tiger pitcher, 1958–67)

Hank was a great left-handed pitcher with several games that came close to no-hitters. Because he was a great pitcher, he wasn't the greatest batter. He would get a roar from the fans if he just got the bat on the ball. Hank and I would use walkie-talkies to talk to each other while traveling on different busses. That was some kind of fun.

Sometimes when Hank pitched, he would refer to the two "midgets" to his right, Dick McAuliffe was on third base and Don Wert on second base. Hank was six feet tall, while Wert was five ten and McAuliffe five eleven." Both "midgets" were real scrappers; they had a lot of energy and liked to fight. We would see dust flying when the runner tried to tag the base where the "midgets" were playing.

Billy Martin (Tiger second baseman, 1958, and manager, 1971–73)

Billy was an over-the-hill player from the New York Yankees when he came to Detroit, but he was the best manager we ever had.

He would go nose-to-nose with any player, umpire, and even the office big shots to get what he wanted. And he usually did.

Bill Norman (Tiger manager, 1958)

Bill was a great manager and would always take the radio crew to lunch, so we loved him. He was fired in 1959 and replaced by Jimmy Dykes.

Rocky "The Rock" Colavito (Tiger outfielder, 1960–63)

The Rock always had a very specific routine when he came to the plate. He muscled the bat behind his head. He also had the best throwing arm in baseball; when a ball came to left field, he could tag out someone at first base.

When we played in New York City, The Rock thrived. One day from left field, he spotted his father being hassled in the stands, so he jumped over the wall and into the stands to lend his father some muscle. No one messed with The Rock. On the road, he and Jim Bunning were the only roommates who would stop and autograph every child's baseball cards and baseballs.

Dick McAuliffe (Tiger shortstop, 1960–73)

Dick was a nice guy and a good hitter. Whenever he would be at bat, he had this strange habit of kicking his leg before he swung the bat. I remember one time in 1968, Dick charged the mound and separated White Sox pitcher Tommy John's shoulder after a pitch almost hit Dick in the head.

Chico Fernandez (Tiger shortstop, 1960–63)

Chico was famous for being the clubhouse jokester. He always made everyone laugh, whether we won or lost a game.

Norm Cash (Tiger first baseman, 1960–74)

Norm was a great guy, always funny and joking around. In 1961, I witnessed the first Detroit Tiger, Norm Cash, hit a ball out of Tiger Stadium.

My sister, Violet, loved Norm. She wanted a souvenir from him so badly. When no one was in the clubhouse, I took his socks and a jersey for my sister. To this day, no one knew it was me, and she was forever grateful.

Bob Scheffing (Tiger manager, 1961–63)

Bob came to the Tigers after Joe Gordon, Billy Hitchcock, Jimmy Dykes, and Bill Norman managed losing seasons. Norman lost his job when the Tigers didn't win twenty games in a row. Scheffing turned it around and won twenty-two games with one loss. He ended the year with 101 victories.

Bob used to bet me that there were no magnolia bushes growing in Boston. He lost and had to pay me the bet with a fresh, new white baseball.

Bill Freehan (Tiger catcher, 1961–76)

Bill was a great ball player and earned a spot on the All-Star Selection eleven times. He then became the head coach of the University of Michigan's baseball team from 1989–1995. He wrote a book, *Behind the Mask*, and I held the microphone as he recorded his memoirs.

Denny McLain (Detroit Tigers Pitcher, 1963–1970)

Denny had a reputation for winning ballgames. In 1968, he was the star—winning thirty games in the regular season. When we were on the airplane or on the bus traveling to and from the games, Denny was the most pleasant to talk to. He was interested in everything and would talk for hours. Good questions or dumb questions, Denny wouldn't care. I could talk to Denny about any subject, and he would make it interesting. In my opinion, he was one of the most knowledgeable, friendly, and outgoing guys you could meet.

One day in Boston we had a bus waiting at the entrance of Fenway Park to take us back to the hotel. I was sitting in a front seat on the bus when Denny came onto the bus and yelled. He wanted my seat. I opened my mouth wide and yelled right back. So loud that my denture fell onto the floor and broke in three pieces. Denny could not stop laughing because when I spoke again, he said I sounded like Donald Duck. Early the next morning, Denny called me and said he had a cab waiting outside to take me to the dentist. When we got there I gave my teeth to the dental technician and he fixed them in ten minutes. He and I both got to the game on time, and the ball club paid the dentist's bill. Denny said, "All's well that ends well." I was very fortunate to have a good friend like Denny.

At the end of that season, Denny McLain won the American League Most Valuable Player Award, an award that was well deserved.

Denny McLain and I meet up again at the reunion of the 1968 World Series team.
Photograph courtesy of Rodney J. Turman.

Don Wert (Tiger third baseman, 1963–70)

Don, like me, was born and raised in Pennsylvania. He was a short man but a good hitter and an excellent runner. In the summer of 1968, he was hit by a baseball in the head while at bat and I remember his helmet shattering to pieces. Don left the game on a stretcher and was never the same.

Chuck Dressen (Tiger manager, 1963–66)

Charlie had a big five-gallon cooking pot and would occasionally make the whole team a delicious pot of stew. Imagine a team manager cooking for his players. This was unheard of, but everyone appreciated his generosity. Even Karen Bush, security guard at the clubhouse door, would enjoy a taste of that stew, which was second to none.

Mickey Lolich (Tiger pitcher, 1963–75)

Mickey brought the World Series home to Detroit in 1968 because of his pitching in the final game against the St. Louis Cardinals. Final score was Tigers 4, Cardinals 1.

Mickey was an outstanding pitcher but even better at playing cribbage. He carried a small board with him wherever he went. Whenever we played, he would win.

Mickey Lolich and I spend some time together again at the reunion of the 1968 Detroit Tigers team Photograph courtesy of Rodney J. Turman.

Willie Horton (Tiger left fielder, 1963–77)

I remember an on-field interview with Willie. It took us two days to get one minute worth of footage of him. He was one of the greatest hitters, and he was also a perfectionist. He was a great Tiger who will always be remembered, as his Detroit Tiger #23 is now forever retired.

Willie Horton and I posing for a picture in the dugout.
Photograph courtesy of Rodney J. Turman.

Gates Brown (Tiger left fielder, 1963–75)

Gates was one of my all-time favorites. On the airplane sitting beside me, he would occasionally steal my meal, and I would go hungry. Now, I love to eat, so for me to let Gates take my food is a symbol of admiration and friendship. Gates, or "Gator" as I liked to call him, played his entire career for the Detroit Tigers.

*Gates Brown and I share some memories of the
old days when he visited the radio booth.
Photograph courtesy of Rodney J. Turman.*

Mickey Stanley (Tiger center fielder, 1964–78)

Mickey was a great ballplayer who eventually became a television broadcaster for the Tigers. I remember during the 1968 World Series season when manager Mayo Smith moved Stanley to shortstop, a move that was a great decision.

*Mickey Stanley was always willing to sign a baseball for me.
Photograph courtesy of Rodney J. Turman.*

Earl Wilson (Tiger pitcher, 1966–70)

Earl was a big man, standing six three and weighing over two hundred pounds. Once, on a bus in Washington, D.C., some kids threw rocks at our bus and broke a window. Glass sprayed over both Earl and I. Neither one of us got mad; we just brushed ourselves off, helped repair the window, and went on our way. If those kids had known how big Earl was, they would have thought twice about throwing those rocks.

Aurelio Rodriguez (Tiger third baseman, 1971–79)

Aurelio's arm was strong, and his precision was unbelievable. Maybe that's why his autograph was so unique and very difficult for anyone to copy. I understand he passed away at the young age of fifty-two in a car accident in Detroit.

Paul Carey (Tiger Broadcaster, 1973–1991)

Paul was the color commentary announcer behind Ernie from 1973–1991. He was quiet and reserved all the time, on the air and off the air. He never criticized a bad play on the field, he just continued calling the game. Sometimes fans would bring presents to the broadcast booth, like a basket of fruit or homemade cookies, and there would always be two, probably one for Ernie and one for Paul, but guess who would take these presents home? Sometimes I would have both of my hands full on the way out of the booth and would say, "Thanks for the presents guys." They were always very generous with me, and I loved the fringe benefits.

Here is a funny story that makes me laugh even today. One time we had a day game at Tiger Stadium. It was about the seventh inning, temperature around eighty-four degrees, and there was no action on the field. Paul normally did the middle three innings, so he was free. He started chatting with a professional photographer that was in our booth, and Paul asked if he would take some pictures. So the photographer took a picture of Ernie and me, and low and behold he caught me sleeping, eyes shut, and my hands on the amplifier knobs like I was working! Even today, when I see Paul he tells me he gets a laugh every time he looks at that picture still hanging on his studio wall.

Paul Carey and Ernie Harwell stand together for a picture during the 1980s.

Sparky Anderson (Tiger manager, (1979–1995)

Sparky had beautiful white hair for his age, and so did I. When I left the parking lot to go home after a game, there would always be kids waiting for players' autographs. When I would drive out, the kids would always scream, "Here comes Sparky." I presumed they wanted his autograph, so I always signed for him. This didn't last long, the kids got wise to me.

Frank Beckmann (Detroit Tiger Announcer, 1995–1998)

The Detroit Tiger radio announcers changed a few times in the 1990s. Ernie and Paul Carey were let go after the 1991 season, and replaced the next year by Rick Rizzs and Bob Rathbun. Then they were replaced at the beginning of the 1995 season by Frank Beckmann and Larry Sorensen (ex-pitcher for the Giants). Frank was one of the best announcers WJR ever had because of his ability to remember facts and tell the radio audience when, what, and where things happened with the Tigers, Lions, the University of Michigan, and all Detroit sports. His recollection of these facts and figures were so correct we even had sports writers checking for accuracy, and Frank was right every time.

One day Frank came up with the idea that he would wear one of the Tigers' baseball gloves while announcing the game to catch any fly ball that would come up by our booth. He had long arms, and even if they did not come into our booth, he would bend over outside the window and try to catch the ball. To this day, I can still see him with a glove on his left hand, a pencil to keep score in his right hand, and his computer up against the left wall for weather and sports information. Once he stopped talking for the commercial break, he would send me out to get him a hot dog, and as usual, I ate two dogs to his one.

What a great career I had working with so many wonderful people. Those were fun times for this engineer!

The following are some of the networks I've worked with:

- I did CBS and Pabst Blue Ribbon Beer with Ted Husing announcing on TV Channel 2.

- CBS was also the outlet for Jackie Gleason and his band of thirty-five people, *Music Under the Stars on Saturday Night*.

- I worked CBS remotes with Edward R. Murrow and Ed Scott, Ed's right hand man. Murrow used to come to

Detroit, especially during the 1950s UAW strike, to interview workers for his *Man on the Street* show.

- For the Canadian hockey broadcasts, I had Foster Hewitt sitting in his booth, right under the big PA speakers, which had music so loud he would pass the word to go to commercial. It was noisy but Foster never missed a play.

- Also with Canadian Hockey broadcasts I handled audio for the Canucks through CKNW and the Calgary Flames through CHQR.

- I did work for all of Israel with Golda Meir. She'd talk to me and we'd confirm that the broadcast came to her "loud and clear."

- Another overseas remote was with a Japanese baseball broadcast. When the star first baseman and the Japanese players had a U.S. tour, I picked them up in Bradenton, Florida, at McKechnie Field. It was an exhibition game with the Pittsburgh Pirates.

- During the 1984 World Series, I got a call to bring my amplifier and mics to Tiger Stadium and feed the whole world in Spanish from Milan, Italy.

I am proud to say more than once I splattered the world with my audio.

During spring training, when I had days off, I had the privilege of working with other teams. Some of the stations and the broadcasters I worked with are the following:

- WCCO Minneapolis with Ray Christenson

- WMAQ Chicago with Lou Boudreau

- WBZ Boston

- KABC Los Angeles

- KMOX St. Louis with Jack Buck and Mike Shannon

- KDKA Pittsburgh with Nelly King and the Gunner

- KNBC Los Angeles
- KSTP Twin Cities
- WCAU Philadelphia with Byron Sam, Richie Ashburn, Harry Kalas, and Chris Wheeler
- WLW Cincinnati with Joe Nuxhall and Branna Man
- WGN Chicago
- CKO Toronto
- CBC Canada Network
- WTOP Washington, D. C.
- MBS, Mutual Broadcasting System in New York City
- WMCA New York City Network

There are others, but I have forgotten them.

More of the following are some of the nicest people I have worked with and the great voices from the past on my mikes:

- Merle Harmon, Kansas City
- Jimmy Dudley, Cleveland and Tigers, when Heilmann got the collapsed lung
- Arch McDonald, Washington Senators
- Paul Howard "Dizzy" Trout, Tigers, and boy could he whistle loudly
- Al Helfer, "Mr. Radio Baseball," Mutual Broadcast Company
- Bailey Goss, television and radio sports announcer for the Orioles, Colts, and Senators, WEEU, Reading Pennsylvania
- Sam Green, sports reporter
- Ed Hayes, sports reporter
- Joe Falls, sports reporter

- Bill White, President of the National League

- Walter Owen "Spike" Briggs, Jr., Tigers' owner

- Dwight D. "Ike" Eisenhower, President of the United States, 1953–1961. He called me by my first name at the Detroit Economic Club.

- Groucho Marx, actor. Representative for Dodge Motors division, interviewed with Jim Sharsmith, radio personality. He gave me a Groucho cigar.

Back when I was growing up on the farm, I never realized the wonderful people I would meet, the great places I would visit, and the impact of radio broadcasting. It still amazes me.

Getting ready to broadcast a Piston's game with Don Wattrick.

Working another Piston's game while employed by WJBK, TV2.

Broadcasting a Detroit Piston's game with Don Wattrick and Paul Carey.

In 1951, broadcasting CBS Pabst Fight Night with Ted Husing and Lenny Pike.

CBS TELEVISION

A Division of Columbia Broadcasting System, Inc.

485 MADISON AVENUE, NEW YORK 22, NEW YORK · PLAZA 5-2000

SEE IT NOW
EDWARD R. MURROW
FRED W. FRIENDLY

February 19, 1952

Dear Lanny:

All of us on "See It Now" want to say
thanks for your cooperation in doing
the Detroit story. Howard Stitzel is
one of the nicest guys I have ever
had the pleasure of working with.
Thanks again to you and your staff.

Cordially,

Edmund Scott

Edmund Scott

Mr. Lanny Pike
Station WJBK,
500 Temple Avenue,
Detroit, Michigan

Even the big cheese from CBS in New York enjoyed my work.

Baseball Traveling Secretaries

I remember the men I met on my travels with the Tigers. They were a unique cast of people, each one a different character all his own. Our secretaries, the ones that traveled with us, were one bunch I especially remember. They would take care of all of our travel arrangements, setting up transportation, room reservations, and sometimes even our entertainment.

Charlie Martin (Tiger traveling secretary, 1948)

Charlie would take care of all of our traveling needs. He would arrange for hotel rooms, transportation, and our bags and equipment while we were traveling. One time in our travels, he didn't pay the bus boys at the railway station for handling our luggage. When we picked up our bags, every bag had been slit with a knife. To this day, I'm still not sure if Charlie forgot to pay or if he was just a tightwad.

Vince Desmond (Tiger traveling secretary, 1950s)

Vince was the smoothest secretary we had in my fifty years. He would walk with us, high hat the players in the bar, but he never took a drink. That's probably because his main duty was to make sure every ballplayer on the team was in bed by midnight.

When we traveled with Vince, everything was free. Tickets for New York shows, the Washington Theater in the Shoreham Hotel, and all of the rides and fees at Disneyland were complimentary when Vince was in charge.

I used to fix televisions for my neighbors, family, and friends. They were the old kind of TVs with tubes and transistors. One time Vince asked me to fix his television. It was a small job; I only had to clean the front switch. Mrs. Desmond asked, "How did you do that so quickly?" I replied, "Well, you just had a dirty front end." Vince laughed until he couldn't catch his breath. I guess I just simply speak my mind.

Charley Creedon (Tiger traveling secretary, 1960s)

Charlie saved our lives one night in Kansas City. After the last game of the series, the team was on the bus headed for the airport. We were behind schedule for our flight and everyone was in a hurry. We actually had two police escorts to get to the airport on time. We drove through red lights and the police said, "Just follow us." We assumed the sirens and flashing lights would stop oncoming traffic, but no. There was a flat, steel-hauling semi truck that was holding eighty tons of steel rods. As we approached a red light, Charlie, Joe Falls, Ernie Harwell, and I all saw the semi truck coming right toward us. Charlie yelled at the bus driver, "Stop, stop, stop!" Luckily, the bus stopped in time, just twelve feet from the steel load. We all owe thanks to Charlie for saving our lives that day in Kansas City.

Charlie was one of the best friends I ever had.

*March 1969, in Lakeland, Florida with Charley Creddon
the Tiger's traveling secretary.*

1967 Detroit Riots

It was during the 1967 season when race riots and pandemonium broke out in downtown Detroit. For the Tigers, we were just finishing a home series when things started to get heated downtown. We were scheduled the next day to have a game in Baltimore, so I decided to leave the broadcast equipment in the booth at Tiger Stadium. I knew I could go and pack my mikes and amplifiers before reporting to the airplane for the next game. That next day, however, the riots started. The city was on fire, and I had to pick up my gear at Tiger Stadium.

My trip on Interstate 75 to the stadium suddenly stopped when I got to the bridge on Fort Street. There were policemen and guards standing in front of my car. They said that the bridge was closed because of the rioting, and they told me to turn around and head back home. I was scheduled to be in Baltimore the next day, and I had to have my equipment! After shivering and shaking in my boots, I came to the biggest decision of my life. I knew I couldn't let the Detroit Tigers organization down, and I was determined to get my gear.

When I got home, I immediately called the stadium clubhouse, and thank goodness, John Hand was there. I explained my dilemma to John, who was the clubhouse boss at the time, and he told me that he could go to the radio booth and pack up my equipment and get it to the bus. That day the greatest man on earth was John Hand. He did a perfect job getting all my equipment into the two cases that I carried to and from all the games. They weighed 185 pounds, and John had it all packed up and in good shape. The next day in Baltimore, I unpacked the cases and saw that I hadn't lost a single microphone, cable, or amplifier, thanks to John, my lifesaver.

In the end, the Boston Red Sox won the 1967 American League Championship. They won because the Tigers lost to the Yankees in the last game of the season in Detroit, which gave the Red Sox one more win than the Tigers. So we were a sorry lot during that winter.

The great news came in 1968, when I got a world championship ring, which I've been bragging about ever since. You see, in 1968 the Detroit Tigers never looked back and won the American League Championship. They went on to beat the St. Louis Cardinals in the seventh game, thanks to Mickey Lolich, the great Detroit Tiger pitcher, who helped us win the World Series. Everyone was in a mass celebration on the airplane, and a great Detroit city parade followed. Detroit was again celebrating unity.

An original 1968 World Series ticket for game 5, the Detroit Tigers versus the St. Louis Cardinals.

A brick at Comerica Park depicting the seven games of the 1968 World Series.

My World Series Ring

I was so happy when I received a 1968 world championship ring. It had a diamond in the center, my name engraved in the side, and a tiger face on it, too. It's the greatest gift one can expect in sports, and that ring gave me bragging rights for life—the life of a farmer, a sailor, and a radio engineer. I never had it appraised for its financial value, but it's worth the world to me. My chest bursts with pride every time I look at it, as I stand up straight when I show it off. It reminds me of captain's inspection on board my old ship—chest out straight, head high, and bubbling over with pride. I think my gift in life has been my ability to pick the best people as friends. When it came to decide who was to get a ring, Jim Campbell said that Ernie, Ray Lane, and I should each be issued World Series championship rings because we were with them as part of the Tiger family. We worked every game as the broadcast team for WJR radio so that the whole state of Michigan could hear the 1968 World Series Champions, the Detroit Tigers.

When it comes to really showing off, I had the privilege to be the Grand Marshal of the Southgate City Parade in 2008. Believe me, I had lots of fun, especially when people yelled for me to show them the ring and up went my hand. We waved and smiled. My wife June, daughter Linda, and great-grandson Jacob were together in the parade, and as we moved along down the street, the people waved some more. I guess I can share the glory that goes along with the championship ring. There's only one thing greater in life than any ring, and that's a happy family.

One of my favorite possessions, my 1968 World Series ring.

My wife, June and I in the Southgate parade.
You can see how proud I am of my ring.

My Day at the Ballpark

In 2010, the boss of the entertainment committee for the Detroit Tigers, Mr. Eli Bagless, called me and said we are going to have a program to honor Ernie Harwell. He said he would like to include me in the ceremony, since I had worked as an engineer with Ernie for a long time. I agreed to come to the ballpark on one condition: I had to have a hot dog as my pay. It is one of my favorite foods; the others are jellybeans and donuts. Back in the day, I was known to eat three hot dogs every game. For the past fifty years, that was my reputation. I didn't work for money; I worked for food!

I arrived at about three o'clock in the afternoon and walked around the front entrance to find the brick dedicated to me by my family. They bought it with the inscription: "Howard Stitzel, WJR Radioman." We then proceeded to the official entrance for the office people and waited to be presented with information. A man arrived and gave us the official Tiger tags showing that we were guests of radio and TV communications. Molly Betensley, Detroit Tigers broadcasting director, came by and said hello, and some of the other office crew stopped and welcomed us. When Eli showed up, his order was, "Let's go to the Tigers home radio booth."

Ten years ago, when I was the boss of the booth, Ernie had been the voice; Price and Dickerson came along later. I used to call Ernie "the kid" in the booth because I was four months older than he was, and in turn we called Jim Price the rookie and Dan Dickerson the baby. I fit right in with them because they always called me "Hungry Howie." Now, as I waited from five p.m. to seven p.m., I moved around and met all my old buddies on the television crews. They kept asking me, "Where's the donuts?" They remembered the times when I would bring donuts and make each engineer eat one. Then Eli came back to the booth and told me to stay in there until 7:10 p.m., which was my time to shine. I tell you I was thrilled to be with the old broadcast voices and stadium biggies. The Tiger games were my life, and to be back with the oldies was a thrill I'll never forget. Thanks to Eli and the Tigers for inviting me to the Ernie Harwell Honor Night. And thanks to the fans that gave me a 35,000-person round of applause.

When my name was announced at Comerica Park, I stood up to wave and couldn't believe how many people were cheering.

So many fond memories of Jim Price and Ernie Harwell.

A gift from my family in 2000, a brick at Comerica Park. Little did they know that someday I would write a book by the same name.

Part 3

My Greatest Loves

My Four Girls

Here is the story of each one of my four girls. These girls are not just girls—they are women, my offspring for three generations. I am so proud of my four girls. There have been many wonderful events and opportunities in their lives; so many, in fact, that there's just not enough space in this whole book to record their successes.

The greatest of my four girls is my wife of sixty-six years, June. Her motto in life is: "Be happy." When we get into spats, she says, "To make me happy again, just before bedtime, a kiss will cure all." I've kept up this routine for sixty-six years. Back when I was at the ballpark, June was the active housewife. She raised our daughter, Linda, to be the wonderful lady she is today. In the meantime, June was good at many sports and activities. She was in a bowling league for many years, yet she never did bowl a three hundred. She also played a mean game of bridge. As a matter of fact, she was a master bridge player. June was so good that she got to go to Las Vegas for tournaments. Her skills fit well into her talents; she even knew how to throw the dice on the craps table. June is the love of my life, and I can still remember the first day I saw her riding on the back of a bread truck in downtown Detroit. I knew then that she was the girl for me.

The next of my four girls is my daughter, Linda. The name, "Linda," means "beauty." But she's not only beautiful; she's smart, too. Linda is an active sports person, loves to travel, and works well with people. She works for Farmers Insurance, and travels north, south, east, west, and all through Michigan. She always gets good results. Linda is also a great golfer, beating her friends because she swings a great driver. One time, Linda came to visit and couldn't wait to tell us her good news on the golf course: she had gotten a hole in one, a once-in-a-lifetime accomplishment. Linda also loves to go to the casinos, when she gets the time, and she always wins. We call her Lucky Linda! We're all proud of you, Linda. Keep it up.

My daughter Linda and I having breakfast together.
She is as beautiful now as she was then.

My first granddaughter is Dr. Jennifer Hammond. What you can't see in this book is how when I think of her, my chest buttons fly off as my whole body stands tall and erect, like I'm going through captain's inspection in the navy again. You can tell how proud I am of her accomplishments. Jennifer is the principal at Grand Blanc High School in Grand Blanc, Michigan, and I can tell you that her whole life is wrapped around school, education, and creating a positive experience for all of her 2,700 students. She wrote her dissertation and we're all so proud of her achievements.

My fourth girl is my granddaughter, Amy Havican. A nurse at Sparrow Hospital in Lansing, Michigan, she's beautiful, smart, compassionate, and helpful to all of her patients. Amy loves her patients, treats them well, does her job, and never complains. She is a great homemaker, a good baker, and a strict disciplinarian at home. Amy's fun loving, but she really is the boss at home. She also loves to golf with her husband, Craig, and tries very hard to beat him, though never to any avail.

I was so healthy during my broadcasting career that I never missed a baseball game in my life until my two granddaughters got married. I would not have missed those occasions for anything. All three girls are married to wonderful men. Linda is married to Harold (Butch) Clarke. He has many shades to his personality. He is kind, a good worker, and can have a conversation on any subject with anyone who's interested. He'll give you his honest opinion and is always right. He's a giant on the golf course as well, but he just cannot bear that Linda got a hole in one before him.

Jennifer is married to Dr. Donald Hammond. He's a super-educator as well and has many thoughts and ideas about helping the youngsters in his classes. Donald is kind, knowledgeable, and a sincere family man. He golfs, too. Donald's always been a fine grandson-in-law and a great man. He teaches ecology and biology at an inner city school in Flint, where he's also a good horticulturist and just loves his students.

Amy is married to Craig Havican, a good golfer who tries to get better every time out on the course. Craig is very honest, a hard worker, likes to talk, and is an excellent father and husband. He works at Sparrow Hospital in Lansing. Passionate with his patients, Craig helps them every step of the way. He's also good at woodworking and home improvement. He knows all about electronics and can work on any computer, large or small. Craig is a great person.

Now I must write about the youngest member of our clan, Mr. Jacob Havican, son of Craig and Amy, and my great-grandson. As I observe his behavior, I can tell that he is wise, smart, and witty. I see a brain in this young man that will help him develop and grow into a wonderful and successful man. I can see him as a ruler of the future, sitting at the head of a conference of world educators. Maybe Jacob will lead all of the nations someday. You know, I am an excellent judge of character.

For the last chapter in my history, I must admit: from growing up as an honest, kind, and sincere boy of the farm in Fleetwood, Pennsylvania, to my fading years here in Southgate, Michigan, I've done everything to the best of my ability. I honor the time I spent in the U.S. Navy and wish every sailor good luck. The navy taught me to follow orders and honor the chain of command. My fondest memories, though, are the years I spent with the Detroit Tigers. They treated me like family, and I am forever indebted to them for a successful career and a lifetime of memories. Of all my experiences, however, none compare to the times I have spent with my own family. They are my lifeline, my loves, and all of my hopes and dreams. My life has been a good one.

This is my family getting ready to celebrate Howard Stitzel Day in Southgate, Michigan.

My wonderful family: Craig Havican, Jacob Havican, Butch Clark, Amy Havican, me, my wife June, Jennifer Hammond, Donald Hammond, and Linda Turman. They are my most cherished part of my life.

● — ● — ● —

Translated from Morse code, means "end of the main message."

CPSIA information can be obtained
at www.ICGtesting.com
Printed in the USA
LVHW101634131122
733028LV00018B/675/J